PattiSmith
A BIOGRAPHY

PattiSmith
A BIOGRAPHY
NICK JOHNSTONE

OMNIBUS PRESS

London / New York / Paris / Sydney / Copenhagen / Berlin / Madrid / Tokyo

Cover designed by Fresh Lemon
Picture research by Jacqui Black

ISBN: 978.1.78038.358.3
Order No: OP54560

Exclusive Distributors
Music Sales Limited,
14/15 Berners Street,
London, W1T 3LJ.

Music Sales Corporation,
257 Park Avenue South,
New York, NY 10010, USA.

Macmillan Distribution Services,
56 Parkwest Drive
Derrimut, Vic 3030,
Australia.

Every effort has been made to trace the copyright holders of the photographs in this book but one or two were unreachable. We would be grateful if the photographers concerned would contact us.

Photo credits: Cover pictures: LFI. All other photos supplied by Mary Evans Picture Library, Mick Gold, Bob Gruen/Star File, LFI, Gerard Malanga, Chuck Pulin/Star File, Rex Features, Donna Santisi & Luciano Viti/Retna.

Typeset by Galleon Typesetting, Ipswich.
Printed in the EU.

A catalogue record for this book is available from the British Library.

Visit Omnibus Press on the web at www.omnibuspress.com

Contents

Acknowledgements

Patti Smith has always measured her own life against the lives of those who have influenced her. One of her life-long heroes has been the French poet Arthur Rimbaud. At a time when Patti was discovering her own identity and writing poetry, and hadn't even considered being in a rock band, she was struck one day by a possible direction: she would write a book about the life and work of Arthur Rimbaud, a man who had inspired her and to whom she wanted to pay tribute by writing a book that took her closer to his myth. The idea passed, but his influence remained in her life.

My idea to write a book about Patti Smith came from a similarly pure motive. I hoped that Patti Smith would be able to collaborate with me on this project but, after a long period of deliberation, her management in New York explained that she would have to decline to participate with the writing of this book.

Close associates explained that the reasons were two-fold. Firstly, she had collaborated with Patricia Morrisroe's Mapplethorpe biography and publicly voiced her disapproval of the finished product and was now generally 'anti-biographers'. Secondly, she didn't want to see a definitive text appear that attempted to categorise her work. Unfortunately, when she declined to assist me in the writing of this book, she also declined on behalf of

John Cale, Tom Verlaine, Jay Dee Daugherty, Lenny Kaye and many others in her immediate circle.

I would, on the other hand, like to extend my gratitude to all those who helped me with the research for this book and to all those (whether quoted or not) who offered their insight into a remarkable story. Special thanks are due to the following people, who spared valuable time to help me: Andreas Brown, D.D. Faye, David Fricke, Gold Mountain, Thurston Moore, Fred Patterson and Lee Ranaldo. I would also like to thank Chris Charlesworth and Omnibus Press for backing this book from the very beginning.

Introduction

IT's freezing cold. The wall is about 15 feet high. Dozens of tiny crosses wave over the top of it. I stand at the entrance to Père-Lachaise cemetery on Rue du Repos in Paris. Patti Smith comes to this cemetery whenever she visits Paris. I follow in her footsteps and walk through the gates and up the Avenue Principale. This is the place where Patti Smith realised that she was an artist.

She had first visited the cemetery in 1969, to pay homage to those she admired. When she returned in summer 1972 she stood over the grave of Jim Morrison, who had died the previous summer, and waited for inspiration to wash over her. Morrison, like Patti, had been obsessed with the French poet Arthur Rimbaud and, in his bid to emulate Rimbaud's romantic myth, had worn out his body and died.

After her trip to Paris in 1969, Patti had returned to New York and continued writing and drawing, beginning to feel that her own work was more valuable than the art of those she hero-worshipped and had fantasised about. Three years later, standing over Jim Morrison's grave, she suddenly realised that she no longer needed to be inspired by him because she now considered herself to be inspired from within. At this point she knew herself and was free to become a poet. This experience in Paris inspired the song 'Break It Up' on her debut album, *Horses*, in 1975.

It is hard to think of a better place for Patti Smith to have discovered herself. The tombs and graves in Père-Lachaise cemetery date back to 1804: some are crumbling, some disintegrating. Statues of angels and saints are worn and stained by the rain. If you find a good vantage point, it sprawls like an ancient village. The Avenue Principale leads to the Monument aux Morts, an imposing mass of stone, surrounded by greenery. The paths to each side twist between seas of graves and names and crypts, with trees and bushes hanging overhead. Hundreds of cats dart about in between the slabs of stone. Patti would have also visited the graves of celebrated writers such as Honoré de Balzac, Guillaume Apollinaire, Colette, Paul Éluard, Marcel Proust and Oscar Wilde. She would have visited the twin grave of artist Amedeo Modigliani and his tragic mistress Jeanne Hébuterne, paying homage to a man whose paintings taught her to celebrate her unusual looks, rather than feel self-conscious. These are some of the artists who encouraged a young Patti to break from the life she saw ahead of her, who showed her how to live, who made her feel that she wasn't an alien. She devoured biographies of these artists, teaching herself and preparing for the life of an artist.

Patti Smith walked offstage from a Patti Smith Group concert to 70,000 people in Florence, Italy on September 10, 1979. Her record *Wave* was the band's most commercially successful album to date. Her four-album career had seen her rise from being a cult writer and poet on the New York art and music scene to become one of the most influential singers in rock'n'roll. She had succeeded in re-defining all the music industry formulas that restricted female artists, setting new precedents for rock literacy. She had found herself revered as a punk poet, a rebel rocker, a feminist icon and a visionary. But a critical backlash had coincided with the release of *Wave* and the tepid reviews reflected Patti's own feeling that the passion had gone. She was tired of the media attention, she was suffering health problems from the pressures of fame and from touring, and she had met the love of her life.

Patti Smith left her rock'n'roll career in September 1979 for an altogether different challenge: in March 1980, she married Fred 'Sonic' Smith, musician and former member of MC5, Ascension and his own Sonic's Rendez-vous Band. The pair set up home in the Detroit suburb of St Clair Shores, Michigan, and effectively retired from music. Women who had projected a powerful feminist image onto her were baffled by Patti's exchange of artistic fame for domesticity and motherhood in the suburbs. But actually Patti Smith had found what she had always wanted: a partner who loved and understood her. She never claimed to be a feminist and her working-class upbringing in rural New Jersey was a source of tradition-alist values. Patti was always searching for answers and in this love she had found one of the most important.

Her self-chosen sabbatical was broken only by 1988's *Dream Of Life* album, a collaboration between her and Fred, received with weak applause by both critics and fans. The album seemed a far cry both musically and lyrically from her debut album, *Horses*, a record that still features in many rock critics' top ten albums of all time.

Horses merged her poetry and rock'n'roll aspirations and was instantly hailed as a classic upon its release in 1975. Patti's tomboy, tough-girl, street-smart image was a striking mixture of Keith Richards, Bob Dylan, French poets Arthur Rimbaud and Charles Baudelaire and French actresses Anna Karina and Jeanne Moreau. She was a femme fatale disguised as a decadent male rocker or romantic poet. Her early poetry smirked at the conventions and boundaries of gender and favoured rock'n'roll rhythms, slang and pop culture references.

Patti had a dazzling array of musical influences which she had nurtured while stranded in New Jersey, including The Rolling Stones, Bob Dylan, The Ronettes, Jim Morrison and The Doors, Jimi Hendrix and Janis Joplin. Aside from Joplin and older legends such as Billie Holiday and Nina Simone, Patti was often frustrated to find that the inspiration she looked for was to be found mostly in male figures. For this reason, she became intrigued by the stories of artists' mistresses and when she left New Jersey for New York City in 1967, her intention was that: to become an artist's mistress.

Patti Smith tore down music and gender conventions by using her poems for lyrics and then pasting them over her band's proto-punk garage rock. And then there was that voice: rich, rasping, simultaneously old and young, a banshee wail, a whisper, fragile, assured, sensuous, confrontational, sexual, defiant, other-worldly, deep, resonant, soulful, timeless, passionate, spooky, beautiful. A cross between Janis Joplin and Billie Holiday.

Her androgynous rebel pose on the sleeve of *Horses* was revolutionary for its time: mocking the tradition of female artists appearing on their record sleeves as either feminised clichés or overt sex objects. When she struck a more typical feminine pose for 1978's *Easter*, it was with unshaven armpits, another symbol of her uncompromising nature.

Patti was also one of the first female artists to challenge her record label and demand to have complete artistic control. This, along with her independently released and self-financed 1974 debut single, 'Hey Joe'/'Piss Factory', and her charismatic personality, did a lot to build her legend as a punk priestess.

Her powerful image and use of ambiguous gender narratives revolutionised the mainstream perceptions of both rock'n'roll and women in rock.

After all this, it is not surprising that so many fans felt betrayed or confused when their spokesperson and female icon retired to get married and start a family, the most stereotypically conventional female role.

The period between *Dream Of Life* (for which there was no tour and virtually no press) and her return to the recording studio in 1995 saw her move from happy suburban life to tragedy. Robert Mapplethorpe, photographer, key friend and influence throughout Patti's life, died of AIDS in March 1989. On November 4, 1994, Fred Smith died of heart failure. Her brother Todd, who had immediately advised her to return to her work as a way of surviving her grief, died one month later of a stroke. And so it was, Patricia Lee Smith arrived at her 48th birthday on December 30, 1994, in a haze of grief.

Shortly before Fred's death, he and Patti had been planning a rock album which was to serve as a noisy comeback. He felt that Patti should reclaim her crown from contemporary artists like Thalia Zedek (singer/ guitarist with Boston-based outfit Come), Liz Phair, P.J. Harvey, Justine Frischmann (of Elastica), Diamanda Galas, The Nymphs, Carla Bozulich (singer/guitarist of Los Angeles band The Geraldine Fibbers) and the entire

Riot Grrrl movement (L7, Bikini Kill, Bratmobile, 7 Year Bitch et al), who had all proclaimed her influence on their work. The album was slated to be recorded during the summer of 1995 and two songs were already written: 'Gone Again' and 'Summer Cannibals'. Fred had also been encouraging Patti to develop her guitar playing and to become more comfortable with writing melodies in addition to chord sequences.

After his death, Patti channelled her tragedy into art and set about recording what would become *Gone Again*, the record which served as an outlet for her stupendous grief. The comeback was high-profile, and alongside the album came a touching book in memory of Robert Mapplethorpe, entitled *The Coral Sea*. In support of *Gone Again*, her celebrated return to live performance saw her explaining the reasons for her 16-year sabbatical at each show: "To many of you I've been out of your eye for a while. And I can only explain that by saying that it was because I was privileged to have been the wife of a great man . . . Fred 'Sonic' Smith."

Sixteen years after her low-key resurrection/final goodbye show in Detroit in June 1980, the house lights dim at the Shepherd's Bush Empire theatre in London. The crowd is packed tight. Uncomfortable older fans who obviously haven't been to a show for some time stand shoulder to shoulder with younger anxious admirers seeing the legend for the first time. Wide-eyed adolescents and early 20-somethings wait to see why R.E.M.'s Michael Stipe, Throwing Muses' Kristin Hersh, Sonic Youth's Thurston Moore and Hole's Courtney Love hold this 49-year-old woman in such high regard.

A roar goes up and Patti appears. She looks gracefully

dishevelled, wearing spectacles and a raggedy old jacket. She has violet socks and silver Dr Marten boots, and is rake thin, her unkempt black hair streaked with the greys of time. After adjusting the reading glasses that sit on the tip of her nose, she holds up a book of her verse and, with manic intensity and emotion begins reciting 'Piss Factory', her first single. All you can see are hundreds of smiling faces. Patti Smith has returned.

1

The Path To New York City

PATRICIA Lee Smith was born on December 30, 1946, on the South Side of Chicago, Illinois, in the aftermath of the Second World War, at a time when most economies were struggling to recover from the damage caused by the conflict. President Roosevelt had died in April 1945 and had been succeeded by Harry Truman. His inauguration took place amid widespread poverty, poor working and living conditions, and the complications of finding employment for 12 million demobilised servicemen.

Grant and Beverly Ann Smith were a conventional working couple. Patti was their first child; a brother called Todd and two sisters, Linda and Kimberly, following her. Grant Smith was a factory worker and Beverly Ann a counter waitress in a drugstore. They were not mystics or beatniks or artists or tortured poets; they were regular working people. In later life, perhaps in a bid to rationalise her own journey, Patti would explain that her father had been a tap dancer and a track star in his youth, and that her mother was a jazz singer.

When Patti was four, her parents moved from Chicago to a new home on Newhall Street on the north side of

Philadelphia. There, her parents encouraged her to be imaginative from an early age: whenever her mother wasn't working she would tell Patti fantasy-laden tales or fairy stories. Her father was constantly reading and absorbing new information, and his inquisitive nature rubbed off on Patti, as she told Dave Marsh in a 1976 interview with *Rolling Stone* magazine: "My dad was equal parts Balenciaga and Hagar the Spaceman in Mega City. My mother taught me fantasy."

This active encouragement helped to develop Patti's imagination, a gift that she would use a great deal later on, concocting countless stories and fantasies for the press. Her parents taught her to seek out the magic in life, to search for the glimmers of brilliance in every dark moment. They encouraged her to find ways to escape the restraints of convention and reality and instead to create her own entertainment.

Patti was born on December 30, under the zodiac sign Capricorn, symbolised by the goat. Most authorities on the general nature of a Capricorn person would list a series of stereotypical traits which actually succeed in fitting Patti's personality and image. Capricorns typically have long noses, dark hair, bony body frames (especially around the knees and elbows), a strong character and are notorious seekers of power. Interestingly, a large number of Capricorns are born into poor families and end up becoming high achievers and attaining considerable wealth. They are often rebellious when young and, on becoming adults, search relentlessly for success and happiness.

Patti was already rejecting the pretty-girl outfits that her classmates wore in favour of her trademark tomboy style and it was already clear that she was never going to be one of the crowd. She always knew deep down that she was from somewhere else. Her time in Philadelphia was plagued by ill health. She contracted rheumatic fever, mumps, chicken pox and double pneumonia. She also had scarlet fever when she was seven which gave her severe hallucinations. She was laid up in her sick bed in front of a coal stove which only exaggerated her feverish visions.

These hallucinations and her mother's love of fantasy were to provide Patti with a wealth of stories, which would later entertain her brother, sisters, fans and the media. The hallucinations terrified her, as they would any child, but later on when Robert Mapplethorpe taught her that they were actually a gift rather than a curse, she realised that she was blessed. She also learned about the fragility of human existence and, as with many sickly children, this later encouraged her to maximise her life.

The only good thing about being a sickly child was that Patti's mother would buy her daughter records as pick-me-up treats. The tradition started when Patti was sick one time and her mother let her choose a record of her choice and Patti chose *Madam Butterfly*. Another record she got when she was ill as a sympathy gift from her mother was John Coltrane's *My Favourite Things*.

She also had what is commonly termed a 'wandering eye' which meant that, due to the laziness of one eye's vision, she had to wear an eye patch. Not only did this exaggerate her alienation from the other kids at school, it also wounded her self-esteem. The eye patch made her look different from the other kids and the more she was teased by school-yard taunts, the more she withdrew into

19

her private belief that she was different from her peers and that there was a reason for that.

When Patti was eight, the Smiths moved to a small development house in Pitman in rural New Jersey. The economy was improving and, having won the 1952 election, Eisenhower had become the first Republican President since 1932. Pitman was flanked by the Jersey shore to the East and industrial flatlands to the West. After her urban life in Philadelphia, the rural nature of Pitman was a shock for Patti; she felt even more isolated than she did in the city. Nearby, there was a swamp and a pig farm.

Her father worked a night shift at the Honeywell Plant and spent most of his free time studying the Bible, gambling or reading about UFOs. Her mother worked all day but still used to take Patti on special trips to Philadelphia, where she would buy her some books or a sandwich. One of the most important parts of Patti's upbringing was the strong sense of family. Her family was her only refuge and when, later on, she turned away from the fame of a rock' n'roll career in order to start a family, the origins of that decision lay back as far as her own childhood. In her mind, everything outside the family home was alien to her.

Patti hated the countryside and spent most of her time with Linda and Todd, writing mini-plays for them to act in and regaling them with fantasy-laden tales. Always tight for money, the Smith children had few toys to play with and no television. Patti and her brother and sister had to find entertainment from within themselves and this further fuelled Patti's mental agility. Patti thought of herself as the aspiring writer Jo March, a character from Louisa M. Alcott's *Little Women* who shared her family struggle to overcome poverty and achieve something in life. This taught her to be independent, a character trait that would lead her later on to move to New York City on her own. In later interviews, Patti said that Jo March was her first influence.

When she was nine, she heard 'The Girl Can't Help It' by Little Richard at a friend's house. The rawness and energy immediately communicated a power that made her whole, told her what it meant to feel entirely alive. This was to prove to be another crucial influence.

Patti's love for music was growing and she now bought records whenever she could. The first record she ever owned was 'Shrimp Boats' by Harry Belafonte. The next was 'The Money Tree' by Patience and Prudence, the third 'Climb Up', a single by Neil Sedaka.

Her parents meanwhile wanted Patti and the family to lead a religious life. Though Patti's reflections on their denomination would later vary from interview to interview, she states on the sleeve notes to *Radio Ethiopia* that she was raised a Christian. She also told one magazine that her father was an atheist and her mother was a devout Catholic, while at the same time recalling to other journalists that her youth was spent with parents who were Jehovah's Witnesses and that she used to ring doorbells on Sunday mornings and hand out copies of their material. This web of conflicting stories is a direct throwback to the young child who was encouraged to use her imagination to create fantasy-based stories.

In 1958, the fourth child, Kimberly Ann Smith, was born. By then, Patti was moving out of being interested in the Jehovah's Witnesses and setting her sights on Buddhism. "I quit the Jehovah's Witnesses," she later told *Newsweek* in 1975, with typical irreverent humour, "because they said the Museum of Modern Art wasn't going to be around after Armageddon."

Her immersion in Buddhism was intensified quite by chance, when she was set a school project in early 1959 which involved each member of the class choosing a country and writing a detailed report about it. Patti chose Tibet. Her teacher told her that she couldn't do Tibet because it was too obscure and because there would be a lack of research material necessary for such a huge project. She insisted and the teacher caved in. Sure enough Patti found it hard to uncover material about Tibet and in her desperation, started praying that something relevant would happen in Tibet, to generate interest. And then, in March 1959, China invaded Tibet and Patti saw the news in the newspaper. Patti said she felt intense Catholic guilt over having prayed for something to happen in Tibet to make it topical for her project. Patti's teacher and class were stunned that her obscure choice of country had become international news.

In 1960, when Patti turned 13, John F. Kennedy reclaimed office for the Democrats and the civil rights movement was able to progress. By then Patti was attending high-school at Deptford Township High School, in New Jersey. It was there that her love of black music grew throughout her adolescent years. Her first boyfriend was a black Jamaican boy – a radical relationship for the times since the civil rights movement had only started to gain momentum during the period 1955–1960 as Martin Luther King, Jr began to campaign for black rights and equality.

Her fixation with fame and glamour revolved around each latest issue of *Vogue* magazine. For a lower-class girl who pretty much lived in a rural area, *Vogue* was a ticket out, a dreamer's manual. Patti took note of the more unusual, skinny models and took comfort knowing that it was all right to look the way she did.

Patti's awkward frame accounted for her extreme self-consciousness around others and on a deeper level, she was still wounded by the eye patch. Her adolescent self-consciousness was partially relieved when her high school art teacher took her to the school library and showed her paintings by the artist Amedeo Modigliani. In an interview with Lisa Robinson for *Hit Parader* in January 1976, she recalled: "I was real impressionable about art . . . I was real self-conscious about being skinny, and I had one teacher who said I shouldn't be. She took me to the school library . . . she was neat . . . and she showed me the Modiglianis and she said I looked like an El Greco or the Blue period or Modigliani." Along with *Vogue*, Modigliani's paintings relieved Patti's insecurities about her body. The paintings were of women with thin, pale angular faces and solemn expressions. Patti immediately identified with these women, thus beginning a life-long association in her mind between feeling good about herself and art. She found approval in art, but not in everyday situations.

Amedeo Modigliani's story is a tragic one. He was born into a Jewish banker's family in Livorno, Italy in 1884. He suffered a sickly childhood, something that for obvious reasons Patti would have related to. He moved to Paris in 1906 and produced sculptures, drawings and paintings at a ferocious pace. He was isolated by his wealthy background but crafted a reputation for himself centred on excessive drinking, drug use and womanising. His art was largely ignored until the final years of his life, as the contemporary success of the Cubists and Futurists rendered his moody portraits outdated, and not progressive enough in style. His life was mostly spent in squalor and poverty, and his minimal income came from selling drawings in cafes or trading small paintings against meals or even a haircut. Modigliani finally started to achieve recognition by the time the First World War was drawing to a close, but he was already physically bankrupt, and worn out by his excessive lifestyle.

His ability to enchant women with his charm, looks, conversation and artistic ability was the talk of Montmartre and Montparnasse, his two haunts. His most celebrated love affair was with Jeanne Hébuterne, who he met in 1917 and with whom he had a daughter. He died of tubercular meningitis in a charity hospital in 1920, having ignored all warnings about his health and Hébuterne, who was pregnant with their second child, committed suicide the following day. They are now buried together in the Père-Lachaise cemetery in Paris.

Patti's discovery of Modigliani's art enabled her to create an entirely new self-image mimicking the women of Modigliani's portraits with their long slender necks, thin pale faces and melancholy air.

The Pitman years were a radical change from Philadelphia, and, unsurprisingly for a rural area surrounded by swamps and farms, there was a tense atmosphere that centred around complicated racial issues. Despite this, Patti kept the company of black students and had a black boyfriend and black friends. She didn't see it as anything unusual and besides, she felt she had more in common with the black students at her high school than the smarter white kids who were inevitably football stars or cheerleaders.

Patti's development as an individual continued to run in proportion to her discovery of new heroes and heroines. And often these heroes and heroines opened doors to new heroes and heroines which is how she discovered Arthur Rimbaud, who would become a dominant influence on her early work. Reading a book about Modigliani, Patti learned that Modigliani had been inspired by the French poets Rimbaud and Charles Baudelaire and rushed off to explore both, sensing that if they had inspired Modigliani, then they would inspire her, too. And so it was, age 16, that Patti bought a Rimbaud book in Philadelphia. For a 16-year-old girl studying in high school and working a part-time factory job, in lower-class New Jersey, the legend of his life must have seemed like the definition of romance.

Arthur Rimbaud was born on October 20, 1854, in Charleville, France. When Arthur was just six years old, his mother was left to raise him and his sisters when her husband Captain Rimbaud abandoned them. Rimbaud was already displaying a natural talent for writing at the age of ten and this had developed by the time he was enrolled at the College de Charleville in 1865. His child-hood was marked by a devout religious fervour but he was questioning and challenging this by the time he declared himself a poet at the age of 15. He devoured French writers such as Rabelais and Hugo and began his quest for the experiences necessary (in his eyes) to become a poet.

At the beginning of September 1870 he was arrested for travelling on a train to Paris with an insufficient ticket and was imprisoned (beginning a chain of parallels with another French writer that Patti devoured, Jean Genet). The arrest led to a string of restless episodes where Rimbaud ran away from Charleville (again something Genet would emulate). By 1871 Rimbaud was holed up in the library in Charleville reading scandalous books about alchemy and magic. It was through these books that he developed his obsessions with the alchemy of the word and set out on his path to use language and words as a means of usurping his earlier faith in God and elevating himself to the position of self-god.

Rimbaud's shift from religious child to revolutionary anti-Christian teenage rebel-poet was sudden and extreme. He began to challenge accepted order, most notably by such acts as writing 'Merde à Dieu' ('Shit to God') on public benches.

Rimbaud wrote a letter on May 15, 1871, which served as a manifesto of his literary intent and is commonly referred to as the *Lettre du Voyant*. Patti was seduced by its content just as Jim Morrison and Bob Dylan were. Rimbaud writes: "The poet makes himself a seer by a long, prodigious, and rational disordering of the senses. Every form of love, of suffering, of madness; he searches himself, he consumes all the poisons in him, and keeps only their quintessences." Parts of Rimbaud's letter are identical to Patti's lifelong friend Robert Mapplethorpe's philosophy on life and his approach to his art: "Let him die charging through those unutterable, unnameable things: other horrible workers will come; they will begin from the horizons where he has succumbed."

By the end of 1871, Rimbaud became close friends with fellow poet Paul Verlaine (whose surname was adopted by Television front man, solo artist and lead guitarist on the *Gone Again* tour, Tom Verlaine), having sent several poems to him. Rimbaud lived with him and his wife in Paris where he developed a taste for smoking hashish and drinking excessive amounts of alcohol, most notably absinthe, a potent green liqueur made from wormwood. This era saw the literal exploration of the ideas laid out in the *Lettre du Voyant* and throughout 1872 Rimbaud worked on the poems that would become *Les Illuminations*. He also travelled with Verlaine to London and Belgium, where they further explored their personal limits but the relationship, which had seen them become lovers, became strained, chiefly because of pressures exerted by Verlaine's wife's family, who attempted to deny Verlaine legal access to his daughter.

Rimbaud returned to his mother's home in Charleville while Verlaine stayed in London, a move that was designed to placate Verlaine's wife. Verlaine fell ill in early 1873 and called for his mother and Rimbaud to visit him. Once he had recovered, his mother returned to France and he and Rimbaud returned to their self-destructive antics. When the relationship became strained again Rimbaud returned to his mother's farm where he began work on his major work, *Une Saison En Enfer*. Verlaine persuaded Rimbaud to return to London yet again in May 1873, but after a series of arguments, he left Rimbaud and went to Brussels. Rimbaud followed him and, in a violent argument there, Verlaine shot Rimbaud in the wrist, an act that led to his imprisonment. Rimbaud recovered on his mother's farm where he wrote the rest of *Une Saison En Enfer*, finished in August 1873.

Une Saison En Enfer's poems are an agonising journey

through Rimbaud's tortured and deranged mind. His grand vision of becoming a god through his art had failed. His disordering of the senses had brought him only suffering and his poetic journey had removed him from his poet's hell and returned him to a search for a sense of God. The end of the collection sees his realisation that now he might "possess truth in a soul and a body". This was Rimbaud's last writing. He was 18 years and ten months old.

By 1874 he had totally renounced literature and disassociated himself from everything he had ever written. When Verlaine succeeded in publishing *Les Illuminations* in 1886, Rimbaud was assumed to be dead. He placed the manuscript with a printer and abandoned its intended form. Rimbaud's proclaimed disinterest and subsequent abandonment of his writings was to make a profound mark on Patti. One could draw a parallel here and say that she was heavily under his spell when she renounced rock'n'roll in 1979.

The next chapter of Rimbaud's life was restless. He travelled ceaselessly, even enlisting in the army at one point, only to desert weeks later (a pattern that would also dominate Jean Genet's life). The places to which he travelled would have captivated the teenage Patti: Egypt, Switzerland, Britain, Cyprus, Germany, Italy, Holland, Denmark and many more. Patti's obsession with Abyssinia (now Ethiopia) sprang from the final chapter of Rimbaud's life, when he took a job with a company that dealt in hides and coffee in Aden in 1880. In December 1880 he went to the company's new trading post in what would become Abyssinia. By 1885 he was living with an Abyssinian woman whom he was rumoured to have married and had begun gun-running, while occasionally returning to work as a buyer at a coffee warehouse. In May 1891 a tumour in his knee necessitated his return to France where, in Marseilles, his right leg was amputated. He died on December 10, 1891, aged 37.

Rimbaud's influence on Patti's life would be enormous. She entitled her early poetry readings, where Lenny Kaye accompanied her on guitar, 'Rock'n'Rimbaud'. She used his name in her nine-minute epic 'Land' on her debut album, *Horses*. She wrote poems about him. She dedicated 'Ethiopia/Abyssinia' on *Radio Ethiopia* to him. In her teens, she so loved and fantasised about Rimbaud, that she later said it was as if he was her boyfriend.

Patti read his work over and over, which helped to numb the drudgery of the part-time factory job she held throughout high school. Rimbaud dominated her artistic aspirations from this point on, the climax of this obsession being when Patti howled his name on *Horses*.

Her next discovery was a predecessor of Rimbaud's, Charles Baudelaire (1821–1867). Baudelaire was another outsider, a poet in exile from society, whose first major collection of verse, *Les Fleurs Du Mal,* was banned on its publication in 1857, on the charge of offending public morality. Rimbaud cited him as a major influence, which surely enticed Patti to read his work. Patti loved literary outlaws and Rimbaud and Baudelaire both had biographies that would guarantee them a lifelong role in the Patti Smith story. Baudelaire devoted his life to literature at the age of 16, which horrified his Paris family. His life was a quest for experience and he travelled, read, frequented prostitutes, used opium and hashish, and had two tortured romantic relationships. The first was with a woman most biographers call Jeanne Duval, the second with Apollonie Sabatier. He read incessantly to train himself for a writer's life – a pattern that Patti adopted: she naturally looked to other artists as teachers and role models. His writing only became known in the 1840s when his family cut off his inheritance and he translated the works of Edgar Allan Poe to support himself. His dark preoccupations with death and love were too strong for the moral concerns of the time: Baudelaire, like Rimbaud, was an outsider, a visionary. His art was banned by society because he was too real, too ahead of his time. Patti loved this romantic idea of an artist suffering outside of society's codes and morals. Baudelaire died when he was 46 in 1867 of syphilitic paralysis (or according to some biographers, a hereditary illness). He was buried in the cemetery in Montparnasse, Paris.

By her last year in high school, she had discovered Bob Dylan, who she thought looked a little like Rimbaud. According to one version of the myth, Patti was sick and at home and her mother was working as a waitress at a drugstore. In the drugstore, they also sold records. Her mother brought home Dylan's *Another Side Of Bob Dylan*, telling Patti that she had no idea who Bob Dylan was, yet somehow based on the cover, how he looked, she figured it was an artist that Patti would doubtless enjoy. She was right. Patti fell head over heels in love with Dylan.

Patti often told her Dylan discovery a different way, saying that she and her mother had a disagreement and to settle the argument, her mother bought her the Dylan album, claiming that she thought Patti would like it because he dressed the same way that she did. Regardless, the story had the same ending: Patti became obsessed with

Bob Dylan, beginning a journey that would eventually lead to her duetting onstage with him in 1995.

She often found herself singing along to songs on the high school bus or dancing to records at parties in other kids' basements. She also belonged to a pair of jazz clubs, where she was introduced to the likes of Thelonius Monk, Miles Davis, John Coltrane and Nina Simone. She would travel by car into Philadelphia with friends to go to jazz clubs like The Showboat and Pep's and also sneak into Baptist churches, where she would listen to the gospel music. The jazz clubs all had an age 18 admission policy, so when Patti heard John Coltrane was going to be playing live in Philadelphia, she dressed specially for the night so she looked older, to try and fool the doormen keeping entry policy that she was not 16, but instead 18. She did manage to get in to see Coltrane – but not for long, since club staff inevitably asked her for I-D and when she couldn't provide any proving she was 18 or older, they asked her to leave. She saw only 15 minutes of the show, but every second of it thrilled her.

Patti claims that her world changed for good when, one Sunday night, late in 1964, her father was watching the *Ed Sullivan Show* and a scruffy bunch of English guys came on singing a song called 'Time Is On My Side'. They were The Rolling Stones and Patti was instantly obsessed. Laughing with *Rolling Stone* in 1976 she said: "Blind love for my father was the first thing I sacrificed to Mick Jagger." 'Time Is On My Side' would be a song that Patti and her band would play repeatedly later on.

Patti gave D.D. Faye, co-editor of Los Angeles-based *Back Door Man* magazine (a lesser known but important title which was launched just before the breaking of punk and folded in 1978) an outline of her rock'n'roll back-ground in an interview which appeared in April 1976: "The only cool music was black: Smokey Robinson, James Brown, John Coltrane. Folk music had some cool people but folk music was too stupid and too creepy. Something cool white had to happen. Then I saw The Rolling Stones on television and I said 'Yeah', 'cause for the first time here was some rock'n'roll guys that I really wanted to fuck. Elvis was too old for me to wanna fuck him and his movies were stupid. If he woulda made good movies, he woulda never have gotten fat. I love 'im though. James Brown made me feel real neat, but a sweaty boxer just isn't my type. With the Stones tho', there was five possible boyfriends. They hit a sexual chord. They talked our language and made it cool to be white. They were like, all those adjectives: dangerous, dirty, bad, ugly, disgusting . . . wonderful . . .

"Anyway, after the Stones came out it was cool to be white. Later on, though, what happened that nobody expected was that Jimi Hendrix came out. I mean, he just shot so far up white girls' asses. He's what wiped out colour for me. When Jimi Hendrix got down, you didn't care what colour he was. Y'know when I was 16 I had this Jamaican boyfriend, and it was real strange. People were all wrapped up in that racial stuff in the early Sixties. Then there was Jimi Hendrix. Now nobody cares. We don't care. There's these weird parallels goin' on in the world. There's still people workin' within their rules and religions and talkin' about races. And it's just a joke to us."

Her connection to the topicality of rock'n'roll began, as Patti read about British music in magazines and learned about the latest happenings in music from WBAI radio.

She discovered Jim Morrison and The Doors, Janis Joplin and Jimi Hendrix, while still maintaining her daily diet of Smokey Robinson and The Ronettes.

Fuelled by fantasies about Rimbaud and Modigliani, Patti decided that she wanted to become an artist. She had excelled in art while in high school and, on the back of her talent, she was offered a partial scholarship to the Philadelphia College of Art, but her parents were unable to afford the rest of the scholarship. So instead, she accepted a freshman scholarship to Glassboro State Teachers' College, where she would start to train to be an art teacher. Her gangly looks (now exaggerated by her insistence on dressing like Greta Garbo) only added to her feelings of alienation. It was a middle-class school and the students were very different from those at Deptford Township High. Patti found that most of them dressed in a similar bland fashion and her Garbo-influenced trench-coats and dark glasses led to her being treated as some-thing of an outsider. By this point she was past caring about belonging and more interested in finding outsider role models who she could latch onto. Her spell at Glassboro was terminated not long before she was set to graduate, because she became pregnant, which forced her to drop out. Abortions were still illegal in 1964 and girls who opted for back-alley abortions often died or became seriously ill. Patti knew that having a child at her age would compromise the rest of her life and leave her trapped in lower-class New Jersey. She decided to have the baby and give it up for adoption, and went to live in New Jersey's Pine Barrens, a deserted suburb, with some friends.

Patti, who had spent most of her adolescence feeling

uncomfortable about the way she looked, now felt worse. She played Dylan's *Blonde On Blonde* double album over and over, listening to his words and daydreaming. Dylan's music would be a crutch that Patti would turn to in another time of crisis in 1994/95. When she gave birth to the child, she gave it up for adoption in nearby Philadelphia, an act that would haunt her for years to come. The experience taught her to value life: resisting the trap of an early motherhood ensured that she would escape the shackles of poverty.

Having lost her scholarship and her child, she started work in a toy factory in Woodbury, South Jersey. The repetition of the work was never relieved by the regular changing of tasks. She claimed that she would have killed herself, had it not meant that she'd miss the next Rolling Stones record. She devoured Dylan, modelling her walk on his in the 1967 D.A. Pennebaker documentary *Don't Look Back*. The factory experience became the inspiration for Patti's debut single, 'Piss Factory', on which she sings, very much in the spirit of Bruce Springsteen, about escaping a life working in a factory for the bright lights of big city life and hopefully, with it, fame and freedom.

And that is exactly what Patti Smith did. She took all of her influences and went to New York City, in search of art and fame and rock'n'roll and the life outside of New Jersey that she had been dreaming of for so long.

2

New York City

PATTI Smith arrived in New York City in spring 1967, with a small pool of cash saved from her factory work and some artists' materials. All she knew was that she wanted to escape New Jersey and her factory job. Her romanticisation of the artist-mistress myth led her to believe that her ambition was to become the tragic mistress of a New York artist. Patti was constantly reading biographies about artists such as Modigliani and their doomed, suffering muse like Jeanne Hébuterne. She wanted to be one of the artists she read about but identified more so with their mistresses.

Her first port of call was the apartment of a New Jersey acquaintance. However, the door was not opened by this acquaintance but instead by a young artist called Robert Mapplethorpe, who had recently moved in. Once Mapplethorpe explained that he didn't know where her friend had moved to, Patti just took off. She spent the first few nights in the city sleeping rough in stations and doorways. This dangerous situation was quickly solved when Patti found work at a bookstore called Brentano's on Fifth Avenue. But although she had found a means by which to support herself, she was still temporarily homeless.

Fate stepped in and had her bump into Mapplethorpe again in Greenwich Village, a chance encounter that turned into a friendship. He took pity on her and invited her to move into his current home in Brooklyn. Mapplethorpe was exploding with creativity and the pair of 20-year-olds were soon babbling enthusiastically about all forms of art. Once Mapplethorpe became aware of the disturbing hallucinations that Patti had suffered since her childhood illnesses, he pushed her to use them as a means of creating art. The visions that had terrified Patti for so long were recontextualised by Mapplethorpe. He taught her not to fear but rather to use them to her creative advantage. Patti began making pencil drawings, thus beginning her journey from wanting to be only an artist's mistress to becoming a recognised artist in her own right.

In November 1967, they moved out of the Brooklyn apartment which they had been sharing with a young couple and into an apartment on Hall Street. The pair commuted from Brooklyn each day to their new jobs at FAO Schwarz, the toy store. This only lasted a short while, for Patti secured yet another job, this time working at Scribner's Bookstore on Fifth Avenue. The bond between them had become very strong and would last right up until Mapplethorpe's death in 1989.

The intensity between the couple made for a period of manic artistic growth and as the friendship grew too large for their small apartment, Patti moved out and into an apartment shared with a young painter. Patti was inspired by the city and often commented on how nobody cared what she wore, a sharp contrast with her New Jersey days, where she had always felt like an outcast. In April 1969 she moved out from her shared apartment with the painter and into an apartment on 12th Street in Greenwich Village, an area much better suited to her artistic drive than Brooklyn. She was still drawing and painting, but was subdued by her discovery of Mapplethorpe's homosexuality.

In May 1969 Patti and her sister Linda took off to Paris. Patti's head was full of Rimbaud and Baudelaire fantasies and Paris provided her with an opportunity to bring her dreams to life. It also offered her the chance to come to terms with all that had happened to her: she had been forced to quit her art teaching course, she had been pregnant, she had given the child up for adoption and she had left her friends and family for New York.

Patti and Linda were aliens in Paris, but as always, their link with civilisation was through the sounds of certain jukeboxes. They met and became involved with a troupe of street singers, mime artists and a fire-eater called Adrillias. Patti and Linda would stand with a hat and collect donations from passers-by. The troupe's territory was between the Dome and the Coupole, but they also visited all the haunts that Patti had read about, especially the cemeteries in Père-Lachaise and Montparnasse.

A huge influence on Patti was the film *One Plus One* by Jean-Luc Godard, a documentary about The Rolling Stones that fused footage of the band recording 'Sympathy For The Devil' with slogans that were chosen by Godard. Patti told *Rolling Stone* in 1976 that: "We were there night and day. We'd come in the morning and watch it over and over and over again, for five days running."

Legendary film director Jean-Luc Godard (b. 1930–) is famed for challenging the conventions of film. He is hailed as the figurehead of the 'French New Wave' film movement in the early Sixties, along with Claude Chabrol and François Truffaut. A slew of classic and idiosyncratic movies during the Sixties such as *À Bout De Souffle*, *Le Petit Soldat*, *Une Femme Est Une Femme*, *Vivre Sa Vie*, *Le Mépris*, *Bande À Part*, *Alphaville*, *Pierrot Le Fou* and *Masculin Feminin*, led Godard to be labelled a cinematic genius. His turbulent marriage to Anna Karina in 1961 inspired many of his earlier movies and she starred in the majority, thus establishing an artist-model relationship that ended in divorce by the mid-late Sixties.

Karina had arrived in Paris in 1961 from her native Copenhagen where she had been a model and an actress in a short film (which had won an award at a festival in Cannes). After meeting her, Godard was smitten with her long dark hair, slim looks, timeless pout and expressive, often melancholic eyes. He failed to persuade her to act in what became *A Bout De Souffle* (*Breathless*) because he was then an unknown. Once this film made him a celebrity, Karina and he married and she starred in most of his films between 1960 and 1966. Their tempestuous relationship led to a messy divorce which was addressed in *Le Mépris* and *Pierrot Le Fou*. With the exception of the controversial and acclaimed *La Religeuse* in 1967, Karina acted in a string of B-movies but largely vanished, leaving her cult status frozen in time.

After 1968's *Weekend*, Godard rejected popular cinema and concentrated his efforts on grass-roots film-making, mostly for political organisations or causes. Moments of sporadic brilliance peppered his work in the Seventies and Eighties (*Hail Mary*, *First Name Carmen*, *Detective*, *Tout Va Bien*, *Passion*) but by and large he transformed himself into a cinematic Bob Dylan, alternately perplexing and dazzling his critics and fans.

One Plus One encouraged Patti's fixation with The Rolling Stones, and in the middle of the sisters' Stones fever, Patti read rumours saying that Brian Jones might leave the band. The extent to which she put her idols on pedestals meant that this news was near catastrophic and, in reaction to it, Patti began to have vivid dreams about Jones.

She once had a minor fan encounter with Jones in 1964 when The Rolling Stones were playing at a high school venue in New Jersey on a bill with Patti Labelle & The Bluebelles. The mood was so calm during Patti Labelle that nobody was dancing, but when The Rolling Stones came onstage, all the girls in the audience began screaming and rushed to the front of the stage. In the crush, Patti, who had a front row seat, was shoved against the stage. At one point, in the manic pushing and shoving, Patti lost her balance and thought she was going to fall under everyone's feet and get trampled, so she reached up to grab at anything to keep her balance and it turned out she had grabbed Brian Jones' ankle. He was playing sitar, sitting on the stage and he kept on playing and stared at Patti as she stared back.

The street troupe relocated to a farm just outside Paris and Patti and Linda went with them. While staying here, a pot of boiling water was accidentally spilled on Patti, who became feverish, in the same way as she had throughout her childhood illnesses. "I was in a lotta pain, had second degree burns or something, all over me, so they gave me belladonna and morphine," she told *Rolling Stone*'s Dave Marsh in 1976. This chemical treatment triggered another vivid dream, which strangely predicted the death of Brian Jones. She awoke from the dream vomiting, and told her sister that they must return to Paris. On their return they saw a headline in a newspaper that they could understand: "Brian Jones Mort".

The premonition profoundly affected Patti, who then started dreaming about her father's heart. This frightened the sisters so much that they vowed to return to Pitman. When they got home they found that their father had suffered a heart attack and was resting in bed. These two incidents shook Patti and she only returned to New York City – in a fragile emotional condition – once her father had recovered. She immediately sought out Mapplethorpe, who was also in a weak condition due to various minor ailments. The couple immediately re-established their friendship and moved into the Chelsea Hotel, with the intention of both becoming famous artists.

The Chelsea Hotel was the perfect habitat for two aspiring artists. Located at 222 West 23rd Street, it had been built in 1884, and was originally a chic apartment block. Among its famous early residents were the writers Mark Twain, Sherwood Anderson and Thomas Wolfe. In 1940 the building was bought by the Bard family and the Chelsea became a mixture of hotel and apartment block. Post-war guests and residents included Dylan Thomas, Brendan Behan, Arthur Miller, William S. Burroughs, Paul Bowles, Willem De Kooning, Roy Lichtenstein, Bette Davis, Henri Cartier-Bresson and Robert Rauschenberg. Stanley Bard took charge of the Chelsea in 1964 after his father's death and a new era began which saw Andy Warhol's entourage arrive en masse. Warhol shot one of his art movies, *Chelsea Girls*, in the hotel and so-called Warhol 'superstars' such as Edie Sedgwick, Viva and Candy Darling moved in. Bard's friendship with rock promoter Bill Graham led to the Chelsea becoming a haven for musicians such as Jimi Hendrix, Frank Zappa, The Band, Janis Joplin and Bob Dylan. The cult of celebrity that grew around the hotel would have strongly attracted Patti, as it gave her the opportunity to play at being famous, while studying those who actually were.

Patti's transition from wanting to be a tragic mistress to aspiring to be an artist soon became evident. She committed herself to writing poems and doing pencil drawings in a notebook that she kept with her at all times. Her friendship with Mapplethorpe had been a catalyst for her, and the more enthusiastic he was about her work, the more she progressed. Her poems from this era were rock'n' roll-influenced and topics unsurprisingly covered such icons as Brian Jones, whose death still saddened her. She would compose poems in the same rhythm as songs by The Rolling Stones, a pastime that became invaluable when she combined poetry with her music.

If Mapplethorpe had been the one who championed her drawings and obsession with art, then it was her meeting with Bob Neuwirth that encouraged her to call herself a writer. Neuwirth was a key figure in the Bob Dylan crowd and Patti knew him only too well from the Dylan documentary *Don't Look Back*. He was also a musician and occasional film-maker and rubbed shoulders with the likes of Jim Morrison. The legend has it that Patti was walking through the lobby of the Chelsea Hotel and a voice called out, asking her where she learned to walk. She turned around to find Neuwirth staring at her. Once she explained that she had picked up Dylan's walk from

Don't Look Back, Neuwirth started up a conversation. He asked what she had in the notebook she was carrying. She said it was full of poems and he asked to read one. He was immediately struck by her style and began from that moment to champion her writing. Patti has often stated that Mapplethorpe introduced her to the idea of being an artist and Neuwirth helped her to become one.

Neuwirth, who was heavily connected to the Chelsea scene, set about introducing Patti to residents such as writer William S. Burroughs and singer Janis Joplin. His influence freed her from being seen as just another groupie, and suddenly she found herself introduced as an aspiring poet. Patti recalled her state of awe in a 1976 interview with *Hit Parader*: "In the space of days I think I had met every rock'n'roll star in New York through Bobby. He tried to open all these doors for me and get my stuff published and he was the one who really pushed me into writing poetry and kept inspiring me to keep the music in the poetry; he said we needed a poet."

When Patti returned to New York after her father's heart attack, she had returned to her job at Scribner's bookstore and her earnings were used to support both her and Mapplethorpe. By the beginning of 1970, she and Mapplethorpe were renting a small studio space at 206 W. 23rd Street for his work. By spring they had moved out of the Chelsea Hotel and into the studio. When Patti wasn't working, she was furiously writing poetry while Mapplethorpe laboured with his art on the other side of the room. The more Patti wrote, the more she developed an understanding of who she was and how she felt. The process helped her to work out some of her identity problems and she gradually began to come to terms with her femininity. Even though her appearance was chiefly based upon male rockers such as Keith Richards and Bob Dylan, she started to seek out a female role model and found the perfect example in French actress Jeanne Moreau.

Jeanne Moreau (b. 1928) graduated from obscure screen and stage roles in the Fifties to become a movie star in Louis Malle's *Ascenseur L'échafaud* and *Les Amants* in 1958. Patti was especially fond of her role in Truffaut's love triangle cult classic, *Jules Et Jim*, in 1961. She told *Circus* magazine that her second album, *Radio Ethiopia*, was: "more like Jeanne Moreau", who she saw as the pinnacle of French femininity: "I've been studying a lot of Jeanne Moreau. She is like so cool. She is sooooo heavy. She's the complete woman."

Alongside her continuing employment at Scribner's bookstore, Patti started spending her lunch breaks at another bookstore, Gotham Book Mart (whose owner Andreas Brown would later publish her poetry). She attended readings there and further fuelled what was now becoming obvious to her: she wanted to be a poet, a sentiment that grew out of her Rimbaud fixation as well as Neuwirth's encouragement. The process of becoming a writer was boosted by her chance meeting with another Chelsea Hotel resident, a young poet called Jim Carroll, who would later shoot to fame with his book *The Basketball Diaries*. He wrote incessantly and so did Patti, leading to a close bond between the two. For a short period during the second half of 1970, Carroll moved into the studio/loft with her and Mapplethorpe. The apartment became the centre of creative overload and one of Mapplethorpe's many creative explosions was to convince

Sandy Daley, a film-maker and Chelsea Hotel resident, to make a short underground film based on an idea he had. The 33-minute result was entitled *Robert Mapplethorpe Having His Nipple Pierced* which, unsurprisingly, showed Mapplethorpe having his nipple pierced. Patti appeared in the black-and-white film wielding a hammer.

For most of 1970, Mapplethorpe and Patti had been regulars at Max's Kansas City, a trendy club-bar-restaurant on Park Avenue South at Union Square. Sandy Daley had introduced them to the hotspot, where the house band was The Velvet Underground, a fact that attracted Patti no end. In between constant trips to Max's and her job at Scribner's, she gave the occasional poetry reading at the Chelsea. She also found a new friend, a fellow New-Jersey rock disciple called Lenny Kaye who worked behind the counter at a record store called Village Oldies on Bleecker Street in Greenwich Village and wrote articles and reviews for music magazines. Patti struck up a conversation with him about an article he had written about doo-wop and Kaye's expert music knowledge and passionate enthusiasm for rock'n'roll immediately endeared him to Patti. Thereafter, she would spend most Saturday nights at the store where they would talk endlessly, listen to records, dance and drink the occasional beer. As soon as it became clear that Kaye could play some basic electric guitar, Patti began fantasising about them making their own music. After Mapplethorpe and Neuwirth, Kaye proved to be the third major catalyst and influence on Patti's life and art.

Around this time, Patti met another Chelsea Hotel figure: playwright Sam Shepard, who encouraged her blossoming writing when he asked her to help co-write a play that became *Mad Dog Blues*. Shepard's rugged qualities and control of language impressed Patti and he became her fourth major real-life influence. Again, she had stumbled upon a person who could encourage and guide her towards her goal. She was still insecure about her talent and unsure exactly how to channel it. Shepard's interest, and especially the collaboration, taught her invaluable lessons about writing.

Once Shepard's influence had made its mark, Patti wanted to celebrate this point in her life by getting her leg tattooed. She had a tattoo of a lightning bolt done by an Italian beatnik woman called Vali, an incident she recounted to *Interview* magazine's Penny Green in 1973: "When she tattooed me, it was painful. It looks like a lightning bolt . . . it was a great turning point in my life because it had come full circle. It had begun as an image and then it had manifested itself in flesh and blood." The tattoo was something Patti needed to do to make the progression of her life seem real, but also to remind her of this magical era.

Her biggest break came when Mapplethorpe asked Gerard Malanga, a poet, photographer and close associate of Andy Warhol's, if he could pull some strings for an aspiring poet he knew who deserved a forum for her work. Malanga's reputation enabled him to arrange for Patti to open for him at St Mark's Church on February 12, 1971. The poetry circuit was anchored around this venue and it was the perfect place for Patti to make her mark. She immediately enlisted Lenny Kaye's help, and he accompanied her on the night on electric guitar. Patti and Lenny opened their set with a cover of 'Mack The Knife' by Brecht, before racing into a string of poems, one of which, 'Oath', would be re-worked to provide the lyric to 'Gloria/In Excelsis Deo'. They also performed an early version of 'Fire Of Unknown Origin' which would surface on the Arista remastered edition of *Easter* as a bonus track in 1996. By the end of the performance, a buzz about an androgynous street-tough New Jersey poet who looked like Keith Richards and had these tough poems and a Rimbaud fixation had already begun. Patti dedicated the evening to French novelist, playwright and occasional film-maker Jean Genet, whose life and art would always have a profound influence on her.

Jean Genet (1910–1986) was born in December 1910 in Paris. His single mother abandoned Genet to the state system in July 1911, where he was delivered to foster parents in Alligny-en-Morvan. The state's arrangement at this time meant that a foster family was paid a monthly fee in return for raising a child until he or she was 13 years old. Genet excelled at his Catholic school until 1924, when in accordance with the contract he was posted to Paris to train as a typographer. From here he ran away, and his lifelong problems began. He was captured and placed into the foster care of a blind composer, and was soon under psychiatric observation, having spent a large sum of the composer's money at a carnival.

He spent 1926 in a pattern that recalled Rimbaud: he escaped, he was caught. He was eventually sent to be a worker on a farm but ran away immediately. On Genet's capture he was condemned to an agricultural penal colony for youths in Mettray, and the imprisonment initiated his belief that he was a terminal outsider, an affront to society. He had been abandoned as a child, introduced to a middle-class family and then abandoned again, and finally placed in a prison. He had also developed a taste for theft while in foster care. The only way a convict could leave Mettray was by enlisting in the army and in doing so, Genet transferred from one all-male authority-driven system to another. He served in the army from 1929 to 1936, then deserted and went on the run, travelling across Europe under various assumed names. In September 1937 he was arrested for theft in Paris and, once he was identified as a deserter, imprisoned in a military prison. The sentence and his army duties ceased when he was discharged for mental imbalance and amorality. He then entered a desperate cycle of theft, capture and imprisonment that lasted for five years. The moment Genet was released from a sentence, he would immediately return to stealing. He increasingly viewed his spells in prison as his only true life, as he felt he was freed of the banality of human existence and able to focus his thoughts.

It was during the early forties that he began to write poems and prose fragments in jail. Between 1942 and 1947 he wrote his five acclaimed novels: *Our Lady Of The Flowers*, *The Miracle Of The Rose*, *Funeral Rites*, *Querelle* and *A Thief's Journal* all of which were based on Mettray; his role as poet, thief (primarily of silk and books), homosexual and outsider; and his endless prison sentences. His myth was cultivated by his biography, these novels and his subsequent friendships with the cream of the Paris intellectual set: Jean Cocteau, Jean-Paul Sartre and Simone de Beauvoir.

His criminal past had caught up with him by the late forties when he was almost sentenced to life imprisonment for earlier crimes, but a personal appearance in court by Cocteau gained him an eventual pardon. Once freed, Genet spent the next decade in a deep depression, writing only a handful of plays and essays: his mythic outcast's role was so real for him, that the cessation of prison spells almost crippled him.

Genet's writing never recovered and, despite the attention heaped on plays he wrote such as *The Balcony* and *The Screens*, he became a French icon primarily for his political activism which centred around supporting extremist political groups such as the Black Panthers, the PLO and the Baader-Meinhof group. His support of such extremists gained him excessive media attention and, mimicking Rimbaud, he spent the years after 1947 dismissing his novels and renouncing literature, a move that Patti would pay close attention to. His final years were spent restlessly travelling like Rimbaud and fighting throat cancer until his death in 1986. He is buried in Morocco.

Patti was fascinated by Genet's life and the fact that most of his novels were partially written in jail. Genet's poetic ancestors were Baudelaire and Rimbaud. He loved the adventurous tales of Rimbaud's life and felt that he too was not a member of society. Patti was open to the romantic–tragic poet myth and Genet was another prime example of a writer whom she elevated to rock star status.

The Genet-dedicated St Mark's reading was a success and Patti continued onwards and upwards. Her next project was a short play entitled *Cowboy Mouth*, which she co-wrote with Sam Shepard. Its subject matter was loosely based on their relationship – it was about a couple who were destined for nothing but a short, intense relationship. They wrote it by pushing a typewriter back and forth across the floor, playing a game of creative ping-pong. The play proved to be the zenith of their short romantic affair and, when it opened at the off-off Broadway American Palace Theatre, they were in effect playing themselves, a situation which was too much for Shepard who quit after the first night, returned to his wife and vanished to London. Patti found out on the play's second night that he had abandoned the play, her and even New York. Her reaction to the rejection was to return to the safe haven of Mapplethorpe's friendship. She was still working at Scribner's but her rock'n'roll aspirations led her to start writing articles and reviews for music magazines and newspapers, no doubt following in Lenny Kaye's footsteps. The first of these music reviews appeared in *Creem* magazine, which had recently taken a gamble and published some of Patti's poems, including 'Oath'. She also appeared in another underground play called *Island*, which had played for some time near the Bowery district. Patti appeared briefly as a speed-freak character.

The St Mark's performance had aroused the interest of a former club owner called Steve Paul, then the manager of albino brothers Johnny and Edgar Winter, two acclaimed blues musicians. He approached Patti with a success plan that included abandoning her beloved poetry and taking up singing. He also insisted that she'd never achieve fame and success with poetry, but only with rock'n'roll. The more he reiterated this fact, the more Patti refused to become what she thought he wanted, which was a bland leather-clad female rock clichéd stereotype. Steve Paul may appear to have an insignificant role in the Patti story, but it was his opinion which once and for all convinced Patti that she was a poet and that if she ever did make a record, it would be on her own terms.

Now that her goals were determined Patti set about fulfilling them. She collated her poetry with the intention of getting it published, while fuelling her rock fantasies by striking up a friendship with Janis Joplin through the Chelsea scene. She also entered into a romantic relationship with Allen Lanier, then playing with an early version of Blue Öyster Cult, who exposed her to the workings of the rock'n'roll industry. He was to become her fifth teacher and influence.

Sandy Daley's short movie *Robert Mapplethorpe Having His Nipple Pierced* was premiered on November 24 at the Museum Of Modern Art. The literal distance between Patti's voiceover and Mapplethorpe's image reflected real-life tension, because Lanier had moved into the loft with Mapplethorpe and Patti. The loft was simply too small for three. Patti was still writing for magazines on a freelance basis though she lost a very short-lived job as staff writer for *Rock* when she sabotaged an interview with Eric Clapton by insisting on asking him what his favourite six colours were over and over again. Her subsequent freelance efforts appeared in *Rolling Stone*, *Rock* and *Creem*, and she often sat up half the night working on her poetry.

By the end of 1971, Patti was more focused and, via the encouragement of other artists and close friends like Mapplethorpe and Lenny Kaye, was able to channel all of her nervous energy into writing poetry. Her tomboy image was now softened as she switched from all-male role models to the Gallic grace of Jeanne Moreau. In short, Patti had found not only a city where she felt finally accepted, but also a group of like-minded individuals. Above all, she had found some acceptance from herself. The year drew to a close with a significant event that confirmed Patti's growth as an artist: Telegraph Books in Philadelphia published her debut collection of poems, entitled *Seventh Heaven*. Gerard Malanga was behind this second big success in Patti's poetry career, just as he had been behind her first high-profile reading. Malanga had been approached by Telegraph Books with a view to putting out a volume of his own poetry. He instead recommended Patti, and Telegraph followed his advice.

Seventh Heaven compiled just under two dozen of Patti's best poems to date, including one dedicated to Marianne Faithfull, another of her heroines. The poems were a clear indication of Patti's personality at this point, mixing gender issues with rock'n'roll. Underlying the 21-poem collection was a quest for identity and self. In 1973 Patti told Penny Green from *Interview* magazine that: "All of these (*Seven Heaven*) poems are about women, seduced, raped . . . me in a male role." The poems played with conventional gender roles, allowing her to adopt a male persona and use a typewriter to explore the boundaries of the self. Her initial years in New York City had been dedicated to self-exploration and learning. Mapplethorpe, Neuwirth, Carroll, Kaye and Shepard were all vital catalysts in Patti's artistic journey. With a foundation of self-definition built, she was now free to discover her true identity.

3

In Search Of Seventh Heaven

NOW that Patti and Allen Lanier had moved out of the tiny studio they had been sharing with Robert Mapplethorpe and into their own small apartment, a period of domestic peace ensued. Patti was living out two paradoxical fantasies at once: she was in theory an artist's mistress, but now also saw herself as a typical female. She told more than one interviewer that her new-found femininity had been nurtured by Lanier and that she finally had some understanding of what it meant to be a woman. On an artistic level, Patti was still refining the developments of the past year and juggling her different creative impulses. She was still writing rock reviews but primarily she was frantically writing more and more poetry. 1972 was the year when she began to wrestle with a choice of direction: poetry or rock'n'roll? On a deeper level she was still unsure if she had the talent to be an artist in her own right and still felt overshadowed by her influences and idols, and those people with whom she surrounded herself.

This specific dilemma was solved by her return trip to Paris in the summer of 1972, when she discovered her artistic self at the Père-Lachaise cemetery standing over Jim Morrison's grave. Feeling equality rather than inferiority before The Doors legend, she knew that she too was now an artist.

Patti returned to New York City and turned the realisations she had had at Père-Lachaise into her second major success as a poet. At the end of 1972, Middle Earth Press published *Kodak*, a slim volume of nine of her poems, including star-heroine tributes to artist Georgia O'Keefe and actress Maria Falconetti.

The second event which would seal the lessons and realisations of Père-Lachaise was a chance encounter with a promoter and booking agent called Jane Friedman. Friedman was a partner in the Wartoke Concern, a publicity firm, and had been responsible for press co-ordination for the Woodstock Festival. At the end of 1972 she was booking acts for the Mercer Arts Center attached to the Broadway Center Hotel on downtown Mercer Street, and ensuring that there was an advance bill for early 1973. Patti seized this opportunity, and tried to persuade Friedman to let her perform at the Mercer, but Friedman was reluctant because she was doubtful that a poet would attract an audience.

Patti persevered. At the beginning of 1973, she was hanging around the Mercer on a regular basis, meeting up with Friedman and, using her swift talk and famous charm, persuaded her to let her open a New York Dolls show. The Mercer was the showcase venue for budding glam-trash acts like the Dolls, and the audience was less than prepared for a poetry reading by a New Jersey girl with a Keith Richards fixation. Despite all this, Patti valiantly won them over. The success of her performance led to Friedman's booking her as the opening slot for other rock bands that played there.

Patti never used a microphone or instrumental backing, but instead read through cupped hands or a megaphone. Her biggest problem was dealing with hecklers, but she generally out-heckled them and won the crowd over. Her successful slots at the Mercer ran up to and during spring 1973. On the strength of these performances and Patti's growing reputation, Friedman agreed to be her manager.

The partnership's first booking was in May 1973, when Patti opened for a singer at a Bleecker Street club called Kenny's Castaways. Fortunately for Patti, the audience included a *Village Voice* critic who called her "a cryptic androgynous Keith Richard look-alike poetess-appliqué". Her mixture of street-tough and bizarre (she often performed at the Mercer with a toy piano tucked under her arm) couldn't fail to gain people's attention.

Throughout 1973 Patti raced flat out to make up for lost time. Among other projects, she modelled furs at a Saks Fifth Avenue fashion show, after which she wrapped a feather boa around herself and sang the oldie 'Baby's Insurance'. Although it seems unlikely that the modern-day Patti Smith would be found modelling furs, at the time it served as another example of an artist who was becoming increasingly comfortable in the spotlight.

Her third book of poetry, *Witt* (pronounced 'white'), was published in September 1973 by Andreas Brown, the owner of New York City's notorious Gotham Book Mart bookstore (a store similar to the Shakespeare And Company bookstore in Paris and City Lights in San Francisco) which has long been the hang-out for famous and aspiring writers and has a reputation for placing literary merit before commercial gain. It was founded in

1920 by Frances Stellof, who on reaching her hundredth birthday on New Year's Eve 1987 received a telegram from (the then) President Reagan congratulating her on "the contribution you have made to our culture".

Andreas Brown bought the store from Stellof in 1967 and continued to uphold the traditions for which it had become famous. Typical of this attitude was Brown's commitment to publishing the poems of the then unknown Patti Smith. He recalls that "Patti was working around the corner . . . I don't remember if it was Scribner's or Brentanos – we did have two large book-stores in close proximity. Actually she was working at Scribner's bookstore on Fifth Avenue, which is now gone, and she used to come and spend her lunch hour here going through our very large poetry section . . . we specialise in poetry and the avant-garde literature kind of scene. And of course she was totally unknown at the time, just a very quiet, very soft spoken young lady and, as fre-quently happens here, young writers will knock on my office door at the back of the store and say that they're interested in finding out how they can get some of their work published . . . whether it's short stories or film treat-ments or poetry or whatever it may be. And because we are traditionally, and have been now for 77 years, a writer's bookstore, going back to the 1920s, a lot of the very famous writers would hang out here and a lot of them still do. The young writers tend to congregate here as well, or aspiring writers as I should say in Patti's case, when she came in late summer 1973. She said that she had written some poems and was trying to find out how she might be able to get them published, and would I look at them? Which is of course not something that I encourage because I have a lot of work to do and no time to read people's manuscripts. But she was very sweet and very shy and so I said, 'All right, leave them with me and I'll look them over during the weekend and see whether I can come up with a suggestion.' And she came back on Monday or Tuesday after the weekend and asked me if I had had a chance to look at them and I said, 'Yes, I've read them and I've found you a publisher already' and she said, 'Who?' and seemed very surprised, and I said, 'The Gotham Book Mart.'

"And she said, 'You're kidding' and I said, 'No, I like your work very much. It's very distinctive and unusual' and indeed it was. And I said, 'If you're willing to work with me on doing some editing and organising of it, I'll be very excited about publishing it.' And we did, and she made it clear to me that she had a distinctive technique of writing and that there weren't errors in punctuation or spacing or anything. This was actually the way she wrote her poetry. In other words, we did a little editorial work on it to polish it, but basically it was published pretty much as she wrote it. It then took a month or so to get it together. And I published it in a fairly modest edition, thinking, you know, 'She's a young up and coming aspiring poet and we'll help her out and just do a little modest book.' I think maybe Patti had done a few readings in peripheral places and I went to a few of her readings after we had done the book. It wasn't a hot best-seller or anything, but before too long she started singing at some of her readings, which she had never done before, at least not to my knowledge. And there was still something very obviously distinct and unique about her, I mean, there wasn't any question about it. The point I'm really making is that when I agreed to do the book it was strictly based on my reaction to the poetry. Her reputation was so minuscule that it certainly wasn't any kind of an entrepreneurial decision on my part. And there was certainly no music involved at all, I mean, she wasn't known as a singer. All of that began to evolve and she was very determined in doing readings and developing her singing abilities and she started getting a following and the thing just escalated. So what just started off, in my intention anyway, as a very modest publishing venture, eventually went into five or seven editions or printings. Eventually it was pirated by somebody in England and somebody in Germany, in other words, they simply took our edition and photocopied it without authorisation and started publishing it, which was a strong indication that she was developing an international following as well."

At the same time, Gotham Book Mart also ran a small exhibit of Patti's drawings in the space on the second floor of the store, also organised by Andreas Brown. "As a result of that book (*Witt*) we became good friends because the book really helped her in a lot of ways," he recalls. "It made what she was writing at that time accessible to people, and I think it probably played a somewhat significant role in the expansion of her reputation and her career. She spent a lot of time in the store and we got to know each other very well, I mean, she's a very charming person to know. She projects an entirely different image, well not so much now, but then, of a really tough kinda hard-rock girl, and she's not that way at all, but of course that's the persona you have to project, I guess. Anyway I found out she was doing drawings and I had a gallery on the second floor and I don't really know who initiated that idea, whether it was Patti or myself, but she must have told me or shown me some of her drawings because I don't know how else I would have known about them. I liked them very much, she's very much in the tradition of Larry Rivers, who comes to mind immediately, but then Hockney as well. These are people who I think had influenced her to a certain extent at that time but it was surprisingly sophisticated and charming artwork. The large pieces are really quite wonderful. We did have an exhibit and it was fairly successful . . . I mean we sold a good number of pieces for her. She's gone on to greater fame, of course, I think the Robert Miller gallery here in New York gave her a major show at one point and that's a very prestigious gallery on 57th Street."

Now that Patti had had three books of poetry published, she decided that for broader appeal and a wider audience she needed to resume her rock'n'roll interests and she called by the Village Oldies store in November to see Lenny Kaye. The pair renewed their friendship and Patti invited him to join her on guitar when she gave a performance at the Les Jardins club. The gig was performed under the moniker 'Rock'n'Rimbaud' and the pair reprised their St Mark's Place set. The success of this set opened up Patti's serious rock'n'roll ambitions and, from this point on, every time she got a gig, Kaye would accompany her on several numbers, using his long-term free jazz interests to create a dialogue between her spontaneity and his improvisation. By the end of 1973, Kaye was an integral part of the act, and random pianists would appear for each gig, fleshing out the sound even more.

The shows continued into 1974 until the pair recruited

a full-time pianist in March, a story which Patti later told *Penthouse* magazine: "At first it was just me and Lenny Kaye farting around at poetry readings. Then it started to gather force. We advertised for a piano player . . . And finally Richard Sohl came in wearing a sailor suit, and he was totally stoned and totally pompous . . . the fuckin' guy could play anything!" Richard 'DNV' Sohl became so named because Patti and Lenny felt that he resembled a character in the movie *Death In Venice*.

Once the trio had established their dynamic, they were itching to record some songs, and with cash from Mapplethorpe and a small amount from Wartoke and from Kaye's own pocket, they booked into Electric Ladyland studios (as a tribute to Hendrix) in New York City on June 5, 1974 to cut a 7″ single which would become 'Hey Joe' (version) /'Piss Factory'. It was produced by Kaye and lead guitar was contributed to 'Hey Joe' by Tom Verlaine, at the time a member of Television.

In retrospect, it was a crucial moment in Patti becoming a punk idol, for this was an independently financed, produced and released single, an unusual move for the times. When punk rock became properly established, a single released in this fashion became a badge of cool and credibility. This 7″ was issued on their own independent label called Mer Records.

The version of 'Hey Joe' was reworked from Hendrix's reading of the rock standard. Verlaine's mangled guitar sounds blended with Sohl's thunderous piano and Kaye's manic strum and, over the top, via Patti's fusion of gender inversion and the focus on Patty Hearst, the song was given a new perspective as the wife-murderer became a female revolutionary. The track was prefaced by a poem called 'Sixty Days' about heiress-turned-hostage-turned-enforced revolutionary Patty Hearst. The highlight of the single, though, was 'Piss Factory' which recounted Patti's teenage experiences as a factory worker, both part-time during her high school days and full-time after her pregnancy. It is a truly groundbreaking and unforgettable song, with Patti reading her prose poem lyric over what sounds like a totally improvised jazzy piece of music by Sohl and Kaye. The song chronicles her factory work in hyper-realistic detail and the final verse is in effect a summary of all she had achieved since leaving New Jersey.

The trio landed a week-long Television support slot at Max's Kansas City for the end of August, which coincided with the release of the single, shows which would help them to develop the future sound of Patti's first LP, *Horses*. They covered Them's 'Gloria' by Van Morrison, with Patti reading her early poem 'Oath' while Kaye and Sohl played the celebrated three-chord sequence beloved of garage bands everywhere. They also covered 'We're Gonna Have A Real Good Time Together' by The Velvet Underground and 'Time Is On My Side' by The Rolling Stones.

The single astonished anybody who had the good fortune to hear it on its release in August 1974. Fred Patterson, who set up *Back Door Man* magazine and was one of Patti's biggest supporters in Los Angeles, remembers this time well: "Every cruise to Hollywood meant a stop at the Tower Records store on Sunset Boulevard. At the time it was simply the best record store in the world for new product. It stocked just about every LP available, including many imports. More importantly, it stocked hundreds of 45s that you just couldn't get anywhere else. It was on one of our visits to Tower that my friend Thom Gardner discovered a record that would change our lives forever. It didn't even have a place in the bins, he found it in the understock that we routinely went through. He turned to me and told me that here was a record by that woman who wrote some cool poetry that ran in *Creem* a few months or so earlier. He handed it to me. To be honest, I didn't remember Patti Smith's poetry in *Creem*, but the producer and guitarist listed on the black label was Lenny Kaye. I knew him as the annotator and compiler of the *Nuggets* collection of Sixties psychedelic punk records and as the writer of the liner notes on a great Eddie Cochran re-issue. If Lenny was involved, it had to have some merit. I grabbed a copy. Thom bought three or four so he could supply our friends like D.D. Faye. When I got home and listened to the record I was quite simply amazed by it. 'Piss Factory' rocked. Not like a Stooges record or a Stones record: it didn't even have a bass player or a drummer on it. The beat was kept up by Richard Sohl's piano playing much like some of those records that Memphis Slim used to make. But more than that, it rocked on visceral and intellectual levels that no one had ever heard before or since. I played it over and over. And its messages of freedom and individuality were definitely things that members of our cult could relate to. It became a great favourite at parties."

D.D. Faye recalls either Gardner or Patterson playing the record to her and several other friends who were writing for Patterson's soon-to-be launched *Back Door Man*: "I first heard about Patti Smith in the fall of 1974 when the 'Piss Factory' single came out and we covered it in *Back Door Man* number 2. We had just started the magazine and I was the co-editor, working with six guys. We sat there and I think we all almost started crying, it was so awesome."

Smith, Kaye and Sohl soon found themselves in California to play a booking at the Whiskey A Go Go club on Sunset Strip in Los Angeles, a show that D.D. Faye remembers to this day: "The next thing Patti, Lenny Kaye and Richard Sohl came and played at the Whiskey A Go Go in Los Angeles and nobody had heard of her and there was hardly anybody there. They did 'We're Gonna Have A Real Good Time Together' and a lot of rock'n' roll covers, and they did a lot of poetry. She did these incredible word jams where she would just improvise. I had heard some jazz before, but it was my first real contact with watching someone improvise. I don't think I've seen anybody do anything similar since – she doesn't do that live any more. She does kind of bits of it, but she used to go on and on. Her frame of reference was amazing because she was so well read. It was so literary and yet rock'n'roll. They were emotional poems, but she also tapped into some psychological symbolism that was kind of psycho-sexual, but it was also involved in American culture. She was not like anybody I'd ever seen before; she was a really powerful person. She was just one of those people who was really charismatic. For those of us who were working towards launching *Back Door Man* – who were intellectual losers who loved rock'n'roll, she was like an alien from Mars, and that's how we felt. Patti introduced me to the power of the word, given in itself and not necessarily backed up by music, because I didn't think of her as a musician, even though the way she could sing was beautiful. With Lenny and Richard playing behind her poetry, I never associated her with the likes of Wordsworth, but after talking to her and interviewing her and listening to her talk about art, it was clear that she was coming from the Beat writers."

The poorly attended gig made a considerable impact on Patterson as well: "That November, the Patti Smith Trio played at the world famous Whiskey A Go Go in Hollywood as the opening act for a band called Fancy (a crummy English band who had a hit with a remake of 'Wild Thing' on the charts). Patti played at least two nights (maybe three) and Fancy did not attract much of a crowd . . . In fact, attendance was so slim that between shows on the first night, security was lax enough for D.D. Faye, me and Thom Gardner to slip backstage and meet and greet Patti and Lenny."

D.D. Faye remembers talking with Patti: "We walked up to her after the Whiskey show and met her, and she was a person of ideas: everything was about writing. Every time she opened her mouth something about poetry or music came out. Every time she spoke she'd be talking about the likes of Rimbaud, Brancusi or Chuck Berry. There was never an emphasis on music or writing, she saw all her influences as the same thing. I think she had her finger on the pulse of something, because of her way of mixing art with sex with rock'n'roll and proclaiming that rock'n'roll was the mixture of art and sex and expressing it that way. Rock'n'roll, especially in America, let loose, in the Fifties, a release of all the puritanical repressed sexual energies, and that's how Patti Smith got into rock'n'roll because she was alienated. However, she knew that there was an energy there and something about her manipulation of that dynamic, of the release of the sexual tension brought about by rock'n'roll, let her release and express the same energy in a different way. She was so in touch with all the cultural references, from Little Richard to Mick Jagger."

Fred Patterson loved the shows: "The first show knocked me out. We stood on the dance floor in front of the stage and watched as Patti, Lenny and Richard blew our minds. Patti danced and strutted around the stage as she sang. Lenny may not be a great guitarist – he'll never be on the cover of *Guitar Player* magazine – but he plays for spiritual, not technical, perfection. Richard Sohl was the rock upon which most of the melody and rhythm of the songs were based. Some of the songs performed were later modified for the first album. Others weren't. I especially remember a great version of The Marvelettes' 'The Hunter Gets Captured By The Game' – a song composed by Smokey Robinson. Between shows Thom and D.D. took me backstage to meet them. I remember Richard being rather quiet, but Patti and Lenny were genuinely interested in us, their fans. They were happy to meet someone in Hollywood they could relate to: someone who knew who The Jesters and The Paragons were, as well as Brian Jones and Jimi Hendrix. I was wearing a 13th Floor Evelators T- shirt that I had hand made. I wore it that night to impress Lenny. It became a topic of conversation. Patti fell in love with it. I promised to make one for her. After the second show we returned to the backstage area where we chatted some more and exchanged addresses. D.D. gave Patti a pair of gloves she was wearing as a way of showing her appreciation for the show. We said our goodbyes and promised to keep in touch as we headed down the stairs. Suddenly, I turned around and went back up the stairs and pulled off my shirt and handed it to Patti and told her to keep it. I told her I wanted to give her something as a small token of thanks for what she and her trio had given my friends that evening."

From the LA show, Patti, Lenny and Richard travelled to a tiny Berkeley record store where Patti was scheduled to give a reading. This in turn led to their playing an audition night at Bill Graham's Winterland in San Francisco, with Velvet Underground fan and leader of The Modern Lovers Jonathan Richman on drums. The addition of drums made it clear that Kaye was having trouble supporting the breadth of their developing sound, so they decided to recruit an additional guitar player.

They placed some ads in the *Village Voice* for another guitarist at the start of 1975, at roughly the same time that Patti sent a letter to Patterson, postmarked January 24, 1975, thanking him for the 13th Floor Elevators T-shirt. She wrote, "I cherish the tee shirt and am the envy of every underdog and sweet scumbag in Metropolis. I think of you guys a lot. It was the highlight of my West Coast tour, having you guys . . . the most . . . wonderful fragile moments. I remember you darting across the street with no shirt on 'cause you gave me yours. Dee Dee giving up her gloves and how glad I was to go buy you guys a few beers. Course I got the dough off of some dumb rich groupie girl but the feel was there."

Patterson tells me, "She went on to answer some questions I asked in my letter to her such as when her next show in Los Angeles will be and about her contribution to a Ray Manzarek solo album. At the end of the letter she wrote: 'I really loved your letter. It was sweet and inspiring. Please write again anytime. You'll be pleased to know I got a haircut sort of like yours. Early Yardbirds. I'm thru with my Stones look. The look for '75 is called HOMELY I ain't putting up with no rock flash shit. It's the era of the space monkey (don't tell anybody that yet 'cause that's gonna be the name of my album), ufo's, dogs, people with jewelled skulls like yourself.' She enclosed a bunch of photographs, some of them autographed; a broadside; a flyer for a gig called Rock'n'Rimbaud III held at Blue Hawaii Discotheque at the Hotel Roosevelt (admission three dollars) on November 10, 1974; the pages of some literary magazine that had an interview with Patti by a "girl from Kalamazoo College"; and a message, two guitar picks and an autograph from Allen Lanier of Blue Öyster Cult. The handwritten message was on a piece of stationery from the Holiday Inn in downtown Toledo and read: 'She's just a dizzy girl, don't pay attention to what she says – she's crazy. She believes in flying saucers – she's nuts – she worships nomads and obscure Eastern religious cults."

Patti, Lenny and Richard played another show as a trio in early 1975, at the St Mark's Church venue in New York, where Patti gave lengthy and assured renditions of 'Piss Factory' and 'Land'. Patti was on a mission which was the sum of all of her influences and she had now elevated art to a life-saving status – after all, it had saved her life, so why couldn't she now save others by introducing them to the healing powers of art? The performance also featured an early version of 'Seven Ways Of Going' which later surfaced on *Wave*. Patti stamped her foot to keep time and wailed what would later be the chorus as if it were an old blues tune.

The auditions for an additional guitarist were painful and, as she later told *Penthouse* magazine, they saw "all sorts of manic baby geniuses from Long Island, kids with $900 guitars who couldn't play anything . . . finally Ivan Kral came in. This little Czechoslovakian would-be rock star." They started playing 'Land Of A Thousand Dances' and Kral just kept playing. To negate the boredom of auditions, they had started playing 'Gloria' with other guitarists and if the auditioning guitarist stopped first, then he wasn't right for the band. Kral kept playing for so long that they hired him. An alternative version of events can be found in Clinton Heylin's book *From The Velvets To The Voidoids*, where it transpires that Kral was actually in Blondie at this time and he quit Blondie for more likely success with Patti's band. Patti sent another letter to Fred Patterson and mentioned the hiring of Kral: "I got a new guy in my group. He's from Czechoslovakia and he plays a hollow body Epiphone."

The first show the quartet played together was at the Main Point Club in Philadelphia, a show which David Fricke, music editor of *Rolling Stone* magazine, helped to organise. He explains, "I was working as a publicist for the Main Point and Eric Burdon was playing, and suddenly the club needed an opening act for the show and a few months before, someone had given me a copy of the 'Piss Factory' single, which had been sent to the club. They'd said 'You'll like this' and I played it, and I was blown away by it. I called her up and they came straight down from New York City and opened for Eric Burdon."

Patti's live performances were becoming more and more charismatic and her ideas about the spaces between crowd and performer were developing, as she later reflected on to D.D. Faye in *Back Door Man* in 1976: "When you immediately take command of an audience, you pull all the punches. Oftentimes I want the show to start with them taking command of me. Then I can see where they're gonna push me. One of the most exciting things about bein' a performer is t'see what they're gonna do to you. It's almost like bein' a human sacrifice. I'm waitin' t'see how they're gonna transform me or make me look like a fool or a demon or an angel. That's why I say stuff like 'What do you want me to do?' 'cause I'm still kinda' new. People will get used to the fact that I'm just as interested in what'll happen during the evening as they are. I'm just as interested to see what kind of trouble we can all get into and then bailout, what kind of heights we can hit. T'see how much mania can be produced. The only way I can gain control over myself is if people, the audience, will lose control. I would rather fail, or have the whole night bomb and have fights break out, than have a bland show. If I'm not communicating with the audience, it's impossible for me to pretend it's not happening."

In March 1975 the band began a joint eight-weekend residency with Television at New York's CBGBs club, an unassuming Bowery bar that was fast becoming the new haunt of the former Mercer Arts Center/Max's Kansas City crowd. The attention that resulted from the shows gave the band the one thing that they desperately wanted and needed: the possibility of a recording contract. The self-released single had been sent out to all the right places and had been brilliantly used as a promotional tool, but now they needed to sign a real record deal. They worked on new songs 'Distant Fingers' and 'Space Monkey' that would surface later on record and the CBGBs stint resulted in some extensive press coverage in *Creem* and the *Village Voice*. At the end of the residency, the band recruited a drummer called Jay Dee Daugherty, who had been in a band called The Mumps and had been recommended by Tom Verlaine.

Fred Patterson received another letter from Patti at this time in response to him sending her the first issue of *Back Door Man*. He says, "Completely inspired by Patti Smith's DIY ethic (and so stated in the first issue) in February of 1975 I began publishing *Back Door Man* magazine. It had Iggy Pop on the front cover. I started it when my friends and I realised that *Creem* wasn't as good as it used to be and we wanted to see bands that we dug get more exposure. My friends were all very articulate about music, so it was easy to get them to write about it. Don, D.D. Faye, Thom Gardner, Bob Meyers, Don Underwood and I were all very passionate about it. Of course I sent the first issue to Patti. I must have also sent her some of the Stooges stationery that I got from Metal Mike Saunders because her next letter (postmarked March 13, 1975) was on it. She said that she loved the magazine and an excerpt of the letter reads, 'let me tell you freddie a lotto great stuff has happened to me in my life but nothing that got me in the heart like you thanking me in *Back Door Man*. to inspire something as cool as that really means something to me. I called to thank you but I got your mom so I hope she gave you the message. she sounded real nice.' She went on to discuss collaborations with Tom Verlaine and Allen Lanier, new material, and that she was being offered record deals by RCA and Clive Davis at Arista. About the latter she wrote: 'don't worry about me signing with a big label. I'll never change, I'll just get better. nobody can change me. I knew who I was when I was seven and I'm still the same.'"

Patti's comments to Patterson are a fascinating insight into the Patti who was on the brink of becoming a star. Everything was about to fall into place for her and he heard from her again. "The next letter I received came in a manila envelope postmarked May 15, 1975. It was addressed to 'you all', and once again she told us how much she loved the magazine and commented on several of its articles (i.e. she asked that Thom Gardner take Clive Davis off a list of people that he had marked for death – because she needs him – though she understood why he would be on it). She told us that she'd help us out any way she could. She even offered to donate a box of 100 'Piss Factory' 45s to us that we can auction off in order to make money to help pay printing costs. This letter was three pages long and handwritten (the other two were typed) and illustrated (i.e. a butt crapping on a Leo Sayer record) and contained more photographs."

A powerful audio document of the pre-drums quartet was made when they played a live set for New York's WBAI radio station. It was the last performance they did without a drummer and their last as an unsigned band. The broadcast went out on May 28, 1975 and captured Patti's sparkling charisma perfectly. It featured Ivan Kral and Lenny Kaye on guitars and 'DNV' Sohl on piano. They opened with a pulsating cover of 'We're Gonna Have A Real Good Time Together' before moving into a lively version of The Marvelettes' 'The Hunter Gets Captured By The Game'. The choice of these two songs reflected the band's traditional rock'n'roll and Motown roots. Patti dedicated 'The Hunter Gets Captured By The Game' to: "Charlotte Rampling and Patty Hearst". Her in-between stories at points made the audience laugh, a trick Patti had picked up from another one of her heroes/influences, television's Johnny Carson.

Alongside an early run at 'Birdland', there were also versions of 'Redondo Beach' and 'Break It Up' that would remain the same when they appeared on *Horses* at the end of the year. Patti's introduction to 'Break It Up' explained that the song had come about from a dream she'd had about visiting Jim Morrison's grave. In the dream, she came across Morrison lying on a marble slab in a clearing in a field of long grass. And Morrison had wings and they were attached to the marble slab, like he was moulded into a sculpture: a monumental grave. And in the dream Patti kept telling him to free himself, by using the words which became the title and chorus of the song.

They also played a rough early version of 'Space Monkey' which reached its crescendo with Patti rapping and the guys making bizarre ape noises. There were also two oldies: 'Snowball' and 'Aisle Of Love', alongside a blistering attack on 'Gloria' complete with a free-form rap by Patti about the power of rock'n'roll and a middle break of 'Land Of A Thousand Dances' which indicated that 'Land' wasn't fully formed yet. They also played versions of 'Piss Factory', 'Distant Fingers' and finally 'Land'. There was no denying that Patti had considerable onstage presence and a great ability to work a crowd. The backing was flawless and imaginative and it was only natural that their sound would attract interested parties.

Record label interest had been developing and, in particular, the quartet had been wooed by Stephen Holden from RCA, who even recorded some aborted demos with the band at the Sixth Avenue RCA studio in February 1975, before spending months deliberating about whether to close a deal or not. *New York Times* music correspondent John Rockwell heard the rumours about the demo and wrote about it, which in turn attracted the attention of Clive Davis, the former President of Columbia Records who was now heading up Arista. Davis lost no time in pursuing and wooing Patti, who was suddenly in the position of being offered contracts by both Arista and RCA. She chose Arista, who recognised her potential as a true artist and promised her total creative control which, at the time, was unusual, if not unheard of. Davis has since claimed that he didn't sign Patti Smith on the strength of the columnist's word, but on the recommendation of his friend Lou Reed. In December 1975, the *New York Times* ran a piece on Patti, quoting her telling Clive Davis during one of their meetings: "I'm not getting any younger. I have to be in a rush – I don't have the strength to take too long becoming a star." Patti was 29 at this point and anxious to make a name for herself before the moment had passed. She signed a six-figure deal with Arista in June 1975. Fred Patterson heard about the deal almost immediately: "Some time after the February letter, I received a postcard from Patti stating that she signed to Arista that day."

One of the first signs that Patti was becoming a real rock star occurred on June 26 when they played the

Other End club in Greenwich Village . . . with Patti's hero Bob Dylan in the audience. There are two myths behind Dylan's appearance. The first suggests that Dylan's coming to the show was quite logical – he wanted to check out this poet–singer who acknowledged him as an influence. The other story is that Dylan turned up as a favour to Clive Davis, who knew that his appearance would guarantee press coverage for Arista's new signing. If this was the case, then it worked, because Paul Williams, the founder of *Crawdaddy* who has since written several acclaimed books about Bob Dylan, was in the audience. Williams was a huge fan of both Dylan and Patti and subsequently a photograph of Dylan and Patti together appeared on the front cover of the Thursday July 3, 1975 issue of the *Soho Weekly News*. Just before Patti and the guys took to the stage for the second set, she was told that Dylan was in the audience. In the piece that accompanied the photograph, Williams wrote: "It put a real nervous edge on everything, which had a powerful effect, she did an even better show than the first one." Patti made various obscure remarks between songs that let Dylan know that she knew he was there. The gig was the first the band had done with a drummer and Dylan's presence was the perfect test for them. After the show he went backstage and Patti was so terrified that one of her heroes had come to meet her that for once she was stuck for words.

Patti told Thurston Moore in a 1996 interview with *BOMB* magazine how she learned Dylan was in the audience and then how he appeared after the show: "He came backstage which was really quite gentlemanly of him. He came over to me and I kept moving around. We were like two pitbulls circling. I was a snotnose. I had a very high concentration of adrenaline. He said to me, 'Any poets around here?' And I said, 'I don't like poetry any more. Poetry sucks!' I really acted like a jerk. I thought, that guy will never talk to me again."

The two sets they played that night were a forum to integrate the long overdue addition of Jay Dee Daugherty on drums and to work over the songs that would define her debut album, *Horses*. It was the beginning of Patti's rapid ascension to fame. Paul Williams was also more than sure that he was watching a woman who was going to be famous: "She's very attractive, in a unique way, she has her own version of the innate androgyny that gave Jagger such power from the beginning. She's going to blow some minds."

Patti's brief dilemma over who should produce the band's debut record came to an end when she and the band settled on John Cale, the former Velvet Underground bass and viola player. Cale had also produced Jonathan Richman & The Modern Lovers, a fact that must have been discussed when Richman had played drums for Patti at the Fillmore show in San Francisco. Recording commenced at Electric Ladyland studios, where Cale turned out to be something of a creative tyrant, as Patti explained to *Rolling Stone* in 1976: "I hired the wrong guy. All I was really looking for was a technical person. Instead, I got a total maniac artist."

Cale began the sessions in August 1975 by challenging the structures of the band's songs and scrutinising every minute detail. The band would later admit that his unusual approach created a specific mood which enabled a song like 'Birdland' to be transformed from a four-minute improvised spoken word rap into a nine-minute epic. The sessions were completed by September 1975 and *Horses* was released in mid-November. In a simple twist of fate, the vinyl disc was manufactured at the Columbia Record Plant in Pitman, New Jersey, where Patti had lived as a child and whose factories had inspired her first recording, 'Piss Factory'.

The advance hype by Arista had been well planned and the record hit the *Billboard* top 50 albums without even a single. Patti Smith's dream had come true – she was going to be a star.

4

Rock'n'Rimbaud

PATTI Smith was 29 when she entered a recording studio with John Cale and re-shaped rock history on *Horses*, a debut that brooks few comparisons. Even today, it is still a record that raises the hairs on the back of your neck, rips your heart out and demands your attention. Lee Ranaldo, solo artist and guitarist/vocalist of New York's highly acclaimed Sonic Youth, sees *Horses* in simple terms: "It's a fucking great rock'n'roll record. The fact is that it incorporated all the best elements of a really good garage band, reaching out and stoking up, and some of the most sophisticated lyric-writing around at the time. Cale's production overlays of various voices added even further to the visionary experience of it. Of course, this record was in some ways a continuation and fulfilment of the lyric pretensions begun by Dylan and Jim Morrison, among others, in their attempt to explode and reinvent rock music in the Sixties. *Horses* is the perfect yet flawed musical child of all that psychedelic Sixties music, coupled with the energy of punk."

Horses features a remarkable black–and–white cover photograph by Robert Mapplethorpe, who managed to capture the soul of the album and Patti's spirit in one image, a photograph taken in the New York apartment of Sam Wagstaff, whose death would be mourned in the 1988 song 'Paths That Cross'.

Typical female artist cover shots at the time would have involved hours in front of a mirror with a make-up team and the clever employment of artificial light to create a soft-focus effect. The artist's spirit or character would be ignored in favour of an image that projected sex-appeal and revealed plenty of flesh. Instead, Patti's hair was unkempt, she wore no make-up and the casually slung jacket over her left shoulder stood as a mock tribute to fellow New Jersey crooner Frank Sinatra. When she draped a man's tie around her neck, she had no idea that 22 years later this exact style would be walking up and down the fashion catwalks at Ann Demeulemeester shows.

Her skintight jeans and white crumpled shirt are a nod to Keith Richards and Bob Dylan. The clothing was distinctly masculine while the slender wrists and positioning of her hands was unmistakably feminine. Arista was perplexed by the choice of a cover shot and objected to her androgynous pose, in particular her visible upper lip hair. Patti refused to airbrush the hair, reminding Arista that she had complete artistic control and that this extended to the work of collaborators such as Mapplethorpe. Her eyes were fixed in a hypnotic gaze, staring straight into the eye of the camera. It was a sensuous come-on, a strong assured look.

In spite of the overwhelmingly masculine influence behind her chosen image, Patti was also trying to pose in a fantasy where she was Anna Karina, the star of those classic early Godard movies. The cover was reluctantly endorsed by Arista and Patti won. Now she had released her own seven-inch single, won creative control from a major record label, and totally rewritten the image of female artists in rock'n'roll.

Horses was released into a musical climate so sterile that the record couldn't fail to impress. As Fred Patterson remembers: "We were into rock'n'roll, our kind of rock'n'roll. For the most part, radio did not help us out. We dug The Stooges, Blue Öyster Cult, Aerosmith, The New York Dolls, Mott The Hoople, The Sweet, Roxy Music, The Velvet Underground, Lou Reed's solo records, as well as old doo-wop, soul music, and rockabilly records. We read *Creem* (especially digging the writing of Lester Bangs) and Nik Cohn's books. We absolutely hated the three Johns of the time: Olivia Newton-John, John Denver and Elton John. We didn't dig The Eagles, Linda Ronstadt, Jackson Browne or other practitioners of the so called Californian rock sound."

Not content with taking on the music industry, sexism, the female image and her new record label, Patti turned her defiant attention towards organised religion, opening her album with a line that snarled youthful independence. Patti took just one sentence to dismiss religion and declare herself the only authority she would recognise. It is a thrilling and rebellious statement and, coupled with the cover image, a perfect introduction to Patti's Rimbaud-fuelled vision.

Patti had already established her reputation on the New York scene as a poet who challenged gender and identity boundaries. She was anti-labels, against the restraints of having to admit that she was 'a woman'. She wanted to be both genders. Her teenage readings of Rimbaud had convinced her that each person contains as much female as

male. She had few female role models and most of those
were tragic victims. When she chose to open her debut
album with a cover version of Van Morrison and Them's
'Gloria (In Excelsis Deo)', it was a glorious mockery of
hairy male rock traditions. Every band in the world with
three chords and cheap guitars played this garage-rock
staple which celebrated male virility and the clichéd male
fantasy of being seduced by a powerful temptress. It
implies simple gratification: anonymous sex. So what
better than to open your album with this rock classic and
re-write the entire meaning by having a strong androgynous woman sing the song. Instead of a male voice
singing about the joys of being seduced by an anonymous
woman, it is altogether more sinister and thrilling: Patti
uses a female voice to sing the male narrator's words. It is
a defiant spit in the face of the boy-girl rock'n'roll pop
song. Because a woman is singing the song, is it transformed into a narrative about lesbian sex? Patti is too
wary of definitions and clear meanings to make it that
easy to define it, and instead the song is anything that the
individual listener wants it to be – male/female or
female/female.

The three-chord strum perfectly suited her band, who
were essentially a tight, raw garage-rock band, adding
further humour to the choice of song: here is a poet-
singer with a reputation for spouting tributes to Rimbaud
and Genet and scores of other artists, and instead of
opening the record with something as literate and breathtaking as 'Birdland', she makes it clear that the listener
must destroy all preconceptions before they are allowed
to appreciate and enter into this work of art. This cover is
the first layer of an intricate unwrapping process which

eventually leads to the naked love song 'Elegie'. Each (carefully considered) part of *Horses* is a layer to be removed until Patti can be stripped bare.

The most striking feature of this debut album is her astonishing voice. It whoops, scrapes, howls, seduces. Her use of intricate phrasings is a direct result of the early Seventies when she was perfecting her poet's delivery and learning from her influences that language is to be played with, teased and re-shaped. Those who did view 'Gloria' as a consummation of desire between two women were aware that Patti was not afraid of turning her listeners on. She was fascinated by eroticism and sex, and often talked of wanting to reclaim pornography as something beautiful rather than something which debased women. The band yanked the original song and shook it up, and the climax of the seduction is everything great rock'n'roll should be: the band are playing as furiously as they can, and Patti is howling and shrieking. When everything gels it is raw, thrilling, stimulating, rendering any other activity or thoughts while you listen pointless. For a band that is using only three guitar chords, they use them well, relying on tempo changes and crescendos for impact. The narrator's adrenaline-soaked focus is on the ringing of bells, an obvious climactic metaphor. It is a moment that achieves what Patti believes: that rock'n'roll can be as powerful as sex, that great rock'n'roll *is* sex.

The listener is given time to recuperate after 'Gloria (In Excelsis Deo)' when the initial splash of cymbal announces the beginning of the light pop reggae of 'Redondo Beach'. The title refers to a beach in California, just along the coast from Los Angeles. The infectious lilt of Lenny Kaye's guitar sits merrily with a reggae-influenced bass line and immaculately thwacked drums. It sounds a bit like a doo-wop song being covered by a drunken calypso band. The lightness of the music is soon undermined by Patti's lyric, which is suddenly revealed to be about a suicide. Two lesbian lovers quarrel and one goes missing. The other woman goes looking for her lover only to find that she has been washed up on Redondo Beach, an apparent suicide victim. The narrative is deliciously elliptical, leaving the listener to figure out why the woman committed suicide.

'Kimberly' is a breathless magical song about Patti's sister of the same name. Patti often talked of her Pitman, New Jersey days and how a barn sat nearby the Smith home. Either in a dream or in reality, the barn burned down after a lightning bolt struck it during a storm. Patti uses this event as the foundation for the song's narrative. The other subject is her sister, who was born when Patti was 11; in the song, Patti combines the storm and the burning barn with her maternal role as her sister's protector. She did play mother to her brother and sisters, so this may well be a true pair of stories. The words fall out of her mouth as she becomes more and more animated, until she is spewing and playing with words like a poet in a moment of divine inspiration. The torrents of images are so visual that the words fuse to provide a wealth of neo-cinematic images, until Patti plays the poet's ace, repetition, in order to get her breath back. Her excitement literally leaves her gasping for air.

Another point where she practically strangles herself to maximise the song's potential is on 'Break It Up', the song which took its origins from Patti's summer 1972 trip to Jim Morrison's grave in Paris. It combines her dream about him where he was trapped in the stone of his own grave and her moment of self-realisation when she knew that she was an artist. The lead guitar is by hired gun Tom Verlaine, whose strangled guitar notes mimic the lyrical struggle to fly again, and the second verse has a bizarre vocal technique where Patti sings while beating her fist on her chest, creating her own version of the cry baby /wah wah guitar effects pedal. It still sounds incredible. Towards the end of the song she strains her voice to the extent that it breaks into a hoarse shout.

'Birdland' opens with a muffled jazzy piano hook that sounds like two-thirds of the 'Gloria' riff – clearly an irresistible inside joke. Patti obviously wasn't joking when she often said that when *Horses* was recorded, they really did only know three chords. As discussed earlier, the song concerns the funeral of Wilhelm Reich and centres its hyper-poetic narrative on Reich's son, Peter, standing at his father's funeral. Lost in youthful confusion and grief, the boy imagines his father coming down in a UFO to swoop him away from the hideous reality of the funeral. The limousines that are gathered around the cemetery during the funeral become UFOs in the boy's imagination. Earlier versions of 'Birdland' only lasted four or five minutes but under John Cale's demented instruction, the song was crafted into a magnificent improvisation that clocked in at nine minutes and 14 seconds. It is a showcase for Sohl's piano skills and Lenny Kaye's piercing guitar, which at one point sounds like a clucking chicken. Primarily it gives Patti free reign to improvise her enthralling narrative and an opportunity to really show off one of rock'n'roll's truly astonishing voices. At points, the improvisational nature is almost detectable, when Patti falters over what the next phrase will be. The UFO hallucination must have come from her father's fascination with UFOs when she was growing up. Fans who had heard the WBAI broadcast were already aware of what the song was about but few would have been prepared for such a breathtaking improvisation of the original idea, almost doubling the earlier version's length. The song has an after-hours jazz-club mood to it, allowing Patti the freedom to draw upon her poetry reading days and let words just dribble out of her mouth. Kaye's guitar feedback is perfect for the thematic disloca-tion that lies at the core of the lyric. The final minute steals from the doo-wop genre but totally deflates any energy, to give the song the sense of a last breath.

One song that wasn't lacking in energy was 'Free Money', a breathless rock'n'roll salute to the rolling guitar sound of Lou Reed and Keith Richards. The chugging drums and guitars were pure garage rock, with Patti yelping and whooping her way through the simple rock lyric, about winning the lottery. At times she sounds uncannily like Lou Reed, peeling off phrases as if from a pocketful of dollar bills. It is the record's most simplistic track, the cries of a woman who grew up in poor New Jersey. It works as a logical partner to 'Piss Factory'.

'Land' is the song that fired up the myth, the song that made Patti Smith as revered as she is today. It is a song that is synonymous with *Horses*. Many people regularly refer to 'Land' as *Horses* – to many fans it *is Horses*. It was the moment when Patti Smith channelled all of her hard training and education into a magical nine minute 26 second explosion of what a rock song should be. It is the blueprint for her unique sound: garage rock and the poetry of Arthur Rimbaud. The band again offer Patti a garage rock classic, 'Land Of A Thousand Dances' (penned by Chris Kenner, turned into a smash hit single by Fats Domino), as the canvas for her visions. The original is used as a foundation upon which the band build and interweave their own textures. Just like 'Gloria', the original acts as a formula glue, holding the idiosyncrasies of the additional song in place. The pulsating introduction gathers momentum as the locker room rape occurs. At exactly the right moment, 'Land Of A Thousand Dances' comes crashing in, predatory and low slung. Amusingly, this original uses a three-chord hook which basically sounds like 'Gloria' at a different pace. It began as a poem in 1973 and evolved into a surging punk-poetry anthem. The hallucinatory images and the scraps of dazzling poetry brought Patti's Rimbaud obsessions into rock'n'roll.

The first of 'Land''s three parts is 'Horses', which begins as a spoken word piece and then develops into a breathless tale set in a locker room. A boy is introduced, drinking tea in the hallway. He is wearing a leather jacket, a rebel rocker, perhaps rather like Mapplethorpe or Marlon Brando. Another (predatory) male appears and violently rapes Johnny up against a locker. The trauma of the experience explodes into Johnny's vision of hundreds of horses. The atmospheric dynamics of the music suddenly rev up into 'Land Of A Thousand Dances', with Patti checking off popular dance manoeuvres. The cover is then used as a canvas for Patti's poetic word-flow. The band break down the tempo and Patti recounts the scene after the rape with Johnny lying on the locker room floor, then defiantly rising and taking off his leather jacket. Assorted knives are reeled off by Patti, all phallic symbols. The rush and surge of the music match her crying out to Arthur Rimbaud. Again, this is a landmark moment in rock history: over a three-chord garage rock anthem, a 29-year-old woman from lower class New Jersey is shrieking the name of a French poet who had died in December 1891. It's an improbable but brilliant pairing.

The passage entitled 'Le Mer De' is a free-form jam over the same three chords. Kaye's guitar sounds like it is galloping. The band simmer down to a restrained hush and Patti breaks into a hallucinatory spoken-word piece about a mare in a forest. The narrator runs his/her hands through the mare's hair and finds a staircase in the horse's mane, then walks up the staircase which leads upwards to a sea. As if to underline the literal meaning of this phrase, a second vocal track is faded in. The next narrative mixes two parallel stories: one features either Johnny committing suicide or the rapist cutting Johnny's throat. Simultaneously, Patti shares one of her old teenage fantasies about Rimbaud. He seduces her, and as Rimbaud and she make love and Johnny dies in a sea of blood, images and symbols of sex and death are poetically offered.

The final rock-out namechecks the Tower of Babel, which was Patti's favourite ranting tool with which to baffle journalists. The Tower of Babel story appears in the Bible in the book of Genesis and recalls how the evolving population of the world built a tower that was intended to stretch towards the heavens as a symbol of human beings' one language and universal similarity. God destroyed the common goal by introducing multiple languages into the crowd, thus offering the biblical explanation as to why there are different languages today. Patti's interest in the story is not unusual for the time, since it tied in with a hippie dream of everyone speaking the same language, a dream of a homogenous society. It was a tale that would surface on the sleeve notes to *Radio Ethiopia*, where she explained her interest in the Tower of Babel as one that equated with her contempt for the acceptance of pre-destined order. The last minute features some dazzling proto-Sonic Youth guitar work by Kaye and then a buried line about leaning on a parking meter. The versions of 'Land' that date back to before the recording of *Horses* would always become entwined in the lyric to 'Gloria' and this subtle cross-reference to 'Gloria' was probably more out of habit than conscious trickery. 'Land' is the point at which rock'n'roll was free to do whatever it pleased. Patti and her band paved the way for dozens of rock experimentalists. In short, if Arthur Rimbaud had been born a century later, he would have formed a band and written a song like this.

The final cut on *Horses*, the last of the layers that Patti had constructed, is 'Elegie', a song co-written with Allen Lanier, who also contributed ghostly guitar to the recording. 'Elegie' is patterned around a mournful piano and an insistent bass guitar. Patti's voice sounds more conventional than at any other point on the album and some of the Bob Dylan-influenced intonation would later resurface as a fixed style on *Gone Again* in 1996. An elegy is defined as a poem that laments a dead person. Some fans believe it is a song for Jimi Hendrix, while others think it is a lament for all of Patti's dead heroes and heroines, which would make a fitting conclusion to her first substantial artistic statement.

Horses has consistently featured in critics' lists of the greatest records of all time. *Spin* magazine's *Alternative Record Guide* listed it as the sixth greatest alternative album of all time. *Big 0* magazine celebrated its tenth anniversary in 1995 by running its list of the Top 100 albums since 1975. It voted *Horses* as the number one album, praising it for "marrying poetry recitation with conventional song structures". When Arista released the record in 1975, it was met with dazzling reviews and sold 80,000 copies in the first five weeks of its release. Arista had done a fantastic job in marketing Patti to the radio stations and media network. It plugged her poet's image and sold the record in advance as a disc that needed only a few plays before the listener fell under its spell. The label respected Patti enough not to follow the easy sales option of presenting her as a female Bob Dylan, and saw her as a valuable asset, in that she was prepared to work as hard as the label. Arista's belief in her talent and in the strength of the record caused it to create a strategic mass-marketing of *Horses* that left all the key buying points in the US salivating in anticipation of hearing and selling this much-talked-about debut album, and the critics in the US and in the UK fell over themselves to toast this ground-breaking debut, again as a result of Arista's PR teams bombarding the important titles and journalists with advance hype.

Charles Shaar Murray, who reviewed it for the *NME* in November 1975, declared it "better than the first Beatles and Stones albums, better than Dylan's first album, as good as The Doors and Who and Hendrix and Velvet Underground albums". In two sentences, he raised Patti above most of her lifelong influences. John

Rockwell, writing for *Rolling Stone*, traced Patti's influences and linked her passion for Jim Morrison, Bob Dylan, The Velvet Underground, Arthur Rimbaud and the Beat poets to his conclusion: "*Horses* is a great record not only because Patti Smith stands alone, but because her uniqueness is lent resonance by the past."

Fred Patterson recalls a crazy encounter with the actor Henry Winkler (aka the Fonz on *Happy Days*) that led to Winkler buying *Horses*. He says, "I can't remember the exact date *Horses* was released but we (*Back Door Man*) loved it. I think D.D. Faye wore out a copy the first week she had it. I remember being at the Tower Records store in Hollywood with my friend Thom Gardner one night when *Horses* was still on display. I watched a fellow wearing a leather jacket (although a square-looking one) pick up the album and ask his friend if he had heard anything about it. I offered that it was a great rock'n'roll record and the guy put it under his arm and took it to the counter. When I walked back to Thom, he said: 'Do you know who that is?' I said: 'No, who?' 'Henry Winkler,' he said. 'Who's that?' I said. 'You know, the Fonz!' I watched so little TV back then that I couldn't recognise the biggest thing on the tube at the time – but I talked him into buying *Horses*!"

As soon as the record was available in November 1975, Patti Smith gave a series of highly quotable interviews with countless magazines, while rehearsing for the band's first tour together. She and her band then played seven blistering sell-out shows at New York's Bottom Line club in December. It was a warm-up for the band, who subsequently embarked on a three-month US tour, on which they aired the debut album and gelled as a group. Paul

Williams, founder of *Crawdaddy* magazine, saw some of the Bottom Line shows. He told me, "I remember being hugely impressed not just by the quality of the music but by the aliveness of it, the way – as with the very best rock'n'roll, and all too rare – you absolutely couldn't know what would happen next, because something powerful was being created at the very moment right before your ears and eyes, as exciting as what you heard last night but also new and very different. Different words to the same songs, different cover songs included, great spontaneous raps and rock gestures between or during songs, all coming from Patti from the point of view of observer but in fact somehow making it a rock experience as opposed to just a poet or poet/singer experience. Intense creative white heat experience. Like The Who or The Doors or The Velvets at their best, for example (and I saw 'em). She was so genuinely excited by the opportunity and circumstances that this art form was giving her to communicate her thoughts/feelings and inspirations to us, the visible audience. I wanted to follow her around and go to a dozen shows in a row . . . I couldn't, but I knew a young woman who did, at a time when that was a most uncommon response to any rock performer." Williams also taps into the qualities that made Patti unique, when he says: 'The marriage of poetic and rock creativity and impulse was so authentic . . . so successful and powerful, that one definitely felt that one was seeing something great that had never been done before – even as she paid homage to great rockers she clearly loved who had come before."

One of the Bottom Line shows had a typical set list for the time, opening with a scorching version of 'We're

Gonna Have A Real Good Time Together', which began with Sohl's boogie-woogie piano introduction and was followed by a band clearly in debt to and in love with The Velvet Underground. The song, which was written by Lou Reed but never recorded by the Velvets, was under-developed enough lyrically to allow Patti to improvise lyrics. Reed became aware that Patti was playing the song live and promptly recorded it for his *Street Hassle* album, anxious to remind everyone that he had written it.

The version of 'Redondo Beach' was faster than on vinyl and more bass-driven, allowing Lenny Kaye's sun-burned reggae licks to surf over the top. 'Free Money' was a little too stoned to be as frantic and charged as it was on record and seemed to delay the full-band frenzy beyond the appropriate point, making the final crescendo appear a little spiritless. The Lou Reed tribute continued with a delicious keyboard-driven take on 'Pale Blue Eyes', which showcased Kaye's stark but luminous guitar playing, even down to the sonic re-creation of a Lou Reed guitar solo. Great renditions of 'Birdland', 'Land' and 'Gloria' sat alongside two garage band staples: the band joyously walk through an uptight version of 'Louie Louie', with Patti's raw voice barking out the chorus, before going into a cover of 'Time Is On My Side' by The Rolling Stones, a song which would always grace their set lists. Patti loved the song because she had listened to it when she felt that her life was passing her by. After all, few women singers in the Seventies were able to launch a rock'n'roll career at the age of 29 and by the time this show was being played she was on the eve of her 30th birthday.

New material such as 'Ask The Angels', 'Space

Monkey' and 'Set Me Free' got its full-band premiere. They often encored with a reckless take on The Who's 'My Generation', a live version of which was recorded at the January 26, 1976 show in Cleveland. The shows highlighted the fact that *Horses* had been recorded by a band that had formed as a full working unit only weeks before they entered the recording studio and, after the first few shows, Patti began to sense that there was more power in the new songs. The tour ended early in 1976 and by then, the songs that would become *Radio Ethiopia* were developing shape. Between the US tour and the Europe and UK tour, a small volume of poetry appeared entitled *The Night*, a collaboration between Patti and Tom Verlaine, who finally got to show off his adopted surname.

Press coverage continued and Patti was giving trademark rants to countless bemused writers, such as D.D. Faye who was treated to several classic Patti Smith monologues when she interviewed her for *Back Door Man* magazine. Fred Patterson was also present, "The Patti Smith group played the Roxy Theater in Hollywood to promote the record. We got to hang with her backstage and D.D. Faye did an interview with her at the Tropicana Motor Inn." The results of this interview ran in the sixth issue of *Back Door Man* in 1976.

The first monologue was about the power of rock'n' roll, where Patti says, "The possibilities of rock'n'roll are gonna start being apparent again. We created rock'n'roll, part of the cycle that's our generation, and our roots have always been heart-oriented and groin-oriented. So, every time rock'n'roll becomes a strong force, something always comes along to fuck it up. People feared Elvis Presley

91

from the waist down, they feared niggers. Anything that was too heavy for 'em they covered up. So instead of listening to Hank Ballard's 'Work With Me Annie', we'd have to listen to 'Dance With Me Henry' . . . I dunno what I'm talkin' about."

Patti was also quick to cite Jimi Hendrix as an example of music transcending the racial barriers of the time, but like all classic Patti monologues, it spirals wildly out of control covering multiple topics: "The people who make the rules are controllin' the world. But it seems funny to me to hear people talkin' about racism and rules when I'm listening to a Jimi Hendrix record. That's why rock'n'roll is so great. It's so above everything. It transcends all the shit. And the great thing is that it's still being born. It's still in its pterodactyl state and has so far to go. I would really like to see rock'n'roll take over the world. Everybody's talkin' about it bein' dead. Alice Cooper . . . here's this jerk-off goin' to Las Vegas. That ain't rock'n'roll. Neither is Captain and Tenille. When people forget, we have to start remindin' 'em again that rock'n'roll is all those adjectives you said, filthy, raunchy and all that and so . . . um . . . It's time for reminders again. When music starts to get creepy there have to be some explosions. Whether it's Sinatra, Presley or the Stones, whoever it is that comes up is more than a bigshot, they're a reminder too. It's almost like when they were buildin' The Tower of Babel . . . this is my favorite rap . . . The Tower of Babel rap. This is my essential rap at this point, so I've given it to other people, but I'll give it to you guys – the best expression of it yet (long pause as she winds up for this one). It's almost like we have some sort of overlord like in The Tower of Babel story. Everyone had telepathy then, they all spoke the

same tongue. So they wanted this spiralling tower up to
the tongue of God. They'd been telepathisising with each
other and now they wanted to go further and have their
tongues join with some bigger tongue. I mean, you
always wanna French-kiss with someone, you never
wanna daddy-kiss. So they were buildin' this tower to get
to the other tongue. But God, or the other tongue, got
scared at the last minute and copped out even though
He'd really wanted to go through with it. It's like UFOs
comin' down and tantalisin' us and then getting scared
and pullin' out. Same thing, God or the Greater Tongue
chickened out at the last minute 'cause it would've been
too heavy like havin' to see himself in a mirror, 'cause
Hog's no heavier than us. We're both pretty heavy,
though. It woulda' been a great confrontation though,
real sexy. But He couldn't deal with it, so He busted up
the Tower of Babel and broke with the telepathy, and
everyone spoke a million different languages . . . In the
Sixties things started pullin' people back to that jello-like
state where we can hit light real fast, with no bullshit
like churches and social orders and stuff. Yeah. The
Jello-light. Yeah sure. In the Sixties they all did it. Everyone that was great . . . Hendrix . . . Morrison . . . And
when everyone died it was like God knockin' down the
Tower of Babel again. It fucked everything up. So we had
to start over again. Only we're much faster movers then
they were thousands of years ago. It used to be that the
evolutionary was every thousand years or so. Now
somethin' happens every ten years. So now it's time. And
all we're doin' is recognisin' the need for somethin' to
happen and doin' somethin' about it. Who knows? We
could be the next Rolling Stones . . . What if Jagger and

Richards had believed that Chuck Berry and Elvis Presley'd been the last ones? Nobody loved Chuck Berry more than Mick Jagger did and nobody loved Elvis Presley more than Bob Dylan. My roots aren't Chuck Berry and Elvis, though. (D.D. Faye was able to make one small comment here: "Yeah but it's all the same roots. You're just translating it for us, our period.") That's why it pisses me off when people say stuff is dead or that it's all been done. They used to say that when I was in art and writin' poetry too. 'Oh, it's all been said.' And I thought that was the funniest thing, because I sure hadn't heard it. I wanna deal with the moment. I'm not satisfied to hear how people did it in history or seein' that The Stones already did it. It ain't enough. We are our own best entertainers."

The final part of this 'rock'n'roll speech' examines where Patti saw her band fitting into the history of rock: "To branch out you gotta have a tree. Our family tree is the people we're discussing. I'm no necrophiliac. I'm not living in a jukebox coffin. All that is behind me and I acknowledge it. It's my heritage. As a performer my family tree is rock'n'roll. By not denying my tree, I keep a grip on its roots. That way I can branch out and blossom . . . from that comes the seeds for other trees. All of this has just been a little fairy tale to make it visual. But I often think of my band as a branch on that tree. We have made a commitment to be a branch."

The band's UK debut was at a venue that had hosted performances by Jimi Hendrix and The Doors, The Roundhouse in North London's Chalk Farm. The dates were Sunday, May 16 and Monday, May 17, 1976. Patti and band also made their British TV debut, on the BBC2 show *The Old Grey Whistle Test*, which aired on Tuesday, May 11. They performed 'Land' and 'Hey Joe'. (During Easter 1976 they had performed 'Gloria' and 'My Generation' on the US show *Saturday Night Live*.)

The short European and UK tour saw shows in places like Amsterdam and Paris, where audiences were treated to 'Pissing In The River', 'Ask The Angels' and 'Ain't It Strange'. Significantly, Richard Sohl decided that he didn't like playing larger concert halls or being on a major international tour, and temporarily left the band. Andy Paley was drafted in to replace Sohl. Paley had been a friend of the band for some time and had played in his own band, The Sidewinders. He had been contacted and had joined for the European shows after only a handful of rehearsals. In support of the tour, Arista put out a 12″ single of 'Gloria (In Excelsis Deo)' backed with the live take of 'My Generation'. The British edition had the expletives edited out – a fact that irritated Patti and led to her later anti-censorship rants. Once the European dates were completed, the band returned to the States, itching to further shape the new songs that would form the basis of the sequel to an astonishing debut album.

5

The Rise And Fall Of Patti Smith

BY the time the band had become The Patti Smith Group, they were spending the remaining part of the summer in New York, recording what would become *Radio Ethiopia*. US fans had been given a taste of what to expect when the band had aired the improvised jam 'Radio Ethiopia' at a performance in New York's Central Park. The album's producer Jack Douglas recorded the whole album in three weeks, including a live take of 'Radio Ethiopia/Abyssinia' on August 9, 1976. Some believe the track and album to be the zenith of the Patti Smith Group's creative efforts; at the time it was quite unusual for the climax of a major label artist's much talked-about second album to be a free-form noise-fest. The speed with which the band fused as a unit enabled them to race out their follow-up.

Radio Ethiopia appeared to run at half the pace of *Horses*. Where *Horses* had shaken the listener with manic fervour, improvised brilliance and barely contained rock energy, *Radio Ethiopia* seemed like a stoned slow-motion ode to Patti's mounting obsessions. The quest for some personal

Patti Smith poses for a portrait in November 1974 in Los Angeles, California. MICHAEL OCHS ARCHIVE/GETTY IMAGES

Sam Shepard and Patti Smith in a performance of the play *Cowboy Mouth*, April 29, 1971, at the American Palace Theatre, NYC. GERARD MALANGA

Patti Smith, hanging out with Iggy Pop and James Williamson of The Stooges in November 1974, backstage at the Whisky a Go Go in Los Angeles, California. MICHAEL OCHS ARCHIVE/GETTY IMAGES

Patti Smith sharing a warm moment with Labelle's Nona Hendryx at a poetry reading at the club, Local, in New York in January 1975. RICHARD E. AARON/REDFERNS

In this 1975 jam, Patti Smith (far right) plays electric guitar while watching John Cale at the microphone. To Patti's right, Tom Verlaine hunches over an acoustic guitar, while Mick Ronson (rear) tunes up. LYNN GOLDSMITH/CORBIS

A brooding portrait of the artist, Robert Mapplethorpe, taken in New York City, 1969 LEEE BLACK CHILDERS/REDFERNS

Bob Dylan sharing an intimate moment with Patti Smith on the stairwell at a party thrown by poet Allen Ginsberg at his home in Greenwich Village, New York City, 1975. KEN REGAN

Patti Smith appearing at The War Is Over rally at Sheeps Meadow in Central Park, New York City, to celebrate the end of the Vietnam War, January 1975. JIM DEMETROPOULOS/RETNA LTD

Patti Smith sitting with Allen Ginsberg at a poetry reading at the club, Local, in New York City in 1975. RICHARD E. AARON/REDFERNS

The Patti Smith Group captured here live in Central Park, July 1976. RICHARD E. AARON/REDFERNS

The Patti Smith Group, (L-R) Lenny Kaye, Richard Sohl, Patti Smith, Ivan Kral and Jay Dee Daugherty, in Copenhagen, Denmark, in May 1976. JORGEN ANGEL/REDFERNS

Patti Smith at a London press conference, October 1976. IAN DICKSON/REX FEATURES

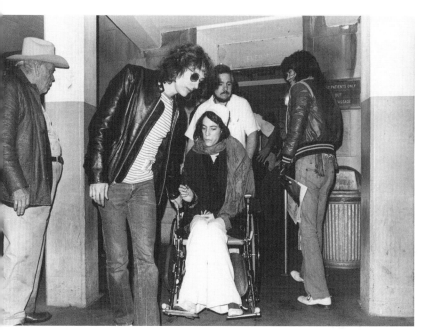

atti Smith is wheeled out of Memorial Hospital of Tampa following a fall during a concert in Tampa, Florida, 1977 LYNN GOLDSMITH/
ORBIS

e Patti Smith Group seen here in January 1977. MICHAEL OCHS ARCHIVE/GETTY IMAGES

Patti Smith wearing a neck brace in 1977, during the six months it took for her to recuperate from falling offstage at her Tampa concert. LYNN GOLDSMITH/CORBIS

peace or the end to spiritual disquiet leaked from every groove. The hesitant voice of *Horses* turned into a frenzied growl. In theory it should have been a record that notched up huge sales: it was a perfect document of the band's sound. The record was also released under the name The Patti Smith Group, signifying the strength of their bond, but the record-buying public didn't share the band's enthusiasm and the album only reached number 122 on the US album charts during the week commencing January 8, 1977, selling a mere 30,000 copies. After the commercial and critical success of *Horses*, it was a disappointment to artist, band and record label.

Robert Mapplethorpe didn't shoot the cover photograph this time; instead it was taken by Judy Linn. The inner sleeve had two photographs taken by Andi Ostrowe on her travels to Ethiopia. Ostrowe was fast becoming Patti's friend and confidante and had volunteered to help the road crew, after talking about her trip to Ethiopia. Another classic shot appeared on the inner sleeve, this time by Lizzy Mercier, featuring a wasted-looking Patti sitting on a street under a graffiti-sprayed wall which reads 'L'Anarchie'. What more needed to be said? The cover photograph seemed to be a slight climbing down after the impact and strength of the Mapplethorpe *Horses* shot. Patti is sitting on the floor of a seedy apartment or hotel room, staring at a point of interest that isn't visible to anyone but her and the photographer. The tones are dark and murky, and Patti's facial expression is quite different compared to the fuck you come-on of *Horses*. The image is also considerably softer and more feminine, and may be seen as Arista's attempt to make it a smash hit record. Despite the cover's deceptive image, the record remains her most difficult and non-commercial, but ultimately her most transcendent rock'n'roll record. Fred Patterson told me he agreed: "It's my favourite of her albums. I love 'Ask The Angels', 'Ain't It Strange' and the epic title track."

The extensive liner notes which Patti dates as having been finished on September 28, 1976 offer additional insight into her mounting obsessions. Her favourite rant and monologue topic had for some time been the Tower of Babel biblical tale and she explains that her identification with the story is based on her dislike of predestination. Patti cites Satan as an artist, the original, the first; then goes on to talk about Jim Morrison's death and the final Doors LP, *LA Woman*. The lengthy passage that follows outlines her fixation with defining an artist, and examines the historical role of the artist as a person exiled from society, or a slave. Patti states that the dilution of the artist came about through artists being too in awe of the church and subsequently being held back by the restrictions of doctrines and dogma. She says that a true artist is a 'nigger' and by nature in opposition to the idea of God. She goes on to explain that these liner notes have been worked on for six months and that now she is heading off to play some shows in Europe.

The final passage recounts how she found a Bible on an aeroplane and began reading the book of *Revelations*, which proves that her constant readings of the Bible were a bid to find the key to conquering either her idea of God or the need for a God. Patti's comprehensive knowledge of the Bible is the result of her endless search for a meaning that would allow her to submit to God. Her rock'n'roll manifesto climaxes with her assertion that she is a true artist and her electric guitar is her mode of artistic expression and her tool of creativity. The album captures an artist torn in half by conflicting desires. On the one hand, she is anxious to pursue the artist's mythical path and reject God and liberate herself from what she believes to be the self-censorship that comes with a religious faith. On the other hand, she is exhausted and tired and wants an end to her self-torment. She wants to submit to her concept of God and relinquish the struggle. One she wants, the other she feels she should want. The songs on *Radio Ethiopia* map out her internal conflict and clear her future path.

The album opens with a Keith Richards influenced guitar riff and tears into an out-and-out rocker ('Ask The Angels') that could have come off any Rolling Stones album during the Seventies. Lyrically and musically it is a celebration, a fist waved in the air – the essence of rock'n'roll. Her indecision about whether she is a poet or a rocker seems to be finally over, the song confirming that Patti now views rock'n'roll as a weapon of revolution.

Popular music had been subjected to a shake-up due to the emergence of punk, which in the UK The Sex Pistols had brought to the media's attention with their lack of respect for authority and theatrical misbehaviour. Patti had seen The Sex Pistols perform when she made her UK debut and wasn't particularly impressed. This was no surprise since their manager Malcolm McLaren had previously lived in New York and managed The New York Dolls, whom Patti had seen many times when she was the opening act at the Mercer Center, albeit long before McLaren became involved with them. Patti had also seen the real thing at CBGBs: Richard Hell when he was with Television and later with The Voidoids. By virtue of emerging around the same time and appearing to disdain the more pompous elements of Seventies rock, Patti, The Ramones, The Clash and The Sex Pistols were bundled together and heralded as the cream of the rising punk scene when, in fact, the music that Patti's band were playing owed more to Sixties garage rock and proto-punk bands like MC5 and The Stooges.

The hypnotic, chant-like 'Ain't It Strange' packs a giant bass drum sound and a mutated reggae beat, producer Jack Douglas effectively capturing the rawness and enormity of the band's live sound. The album is clearly the work of a band who had been touring heavily, unlike the sound of *Horses* which was recorded by a band whose brief incarnation had been developed in small clubs. 'Ain't It Strange' opens with a scene that could have come out of a low-budget movie: a girl in a white dress and a boy who's obviously shooting up drugs. The visual associations are sleazy, even sordid. The break, about two and a half minutes into the song, offers one of Patti's most emotional vocal performances. The circular beat adds a sense of primitive dance, an attempt to communicate with a higher being or spirit, the quest for another dimension. As the frenzy of the song's chants gather, Patti's shredded hoarse voice cries for God to make a gesture, a move. It is one of many moments on the album where Patti calls for God to appear, to show himself. She is partly challenging her notions of a God and partly asking for God to appear and appease her spiritual restlessness. She isn't the first and won't be the last artist to be tormented by a concept of God which defies rational belief and lacks tangible comprehension. In short, she is improvising on the subject matter of Rimbaud's *Une Saison En Enfer.*

'Poppies' is listed on the inner sleeve as having been inspired by Jim Morrison, Edie Sedgwick and the Queen Of Sheba, a typically extreme and diverse cocktail of Patti idols. The lyrics primarily concern the life and times of Sedgwick, whose grace, sophistication, fame, wealth and tragic early demise were more than enough to elevate her into Patti's Hall Of Fame.

Edie Sedgwick (1943–1971) was the most notorious of Andy Warhol's so-called 'superstars'. Born into an old-money New England family, she was one of eight children whose parents raised her and the rest of the family on a ranch in Santa Barbara, California. Edie was a fragile, vulnerable child who showed the first signs of a troubled personality when she was admitted into hospital at the age of 13, suffering from anorexia nervosa. By the time she was 19, her father had committed her to a psychiatric hospital. She spent a year in two different hospitals and, on her release, became pregnant. Edie had an abortion and in 1963 moved to Cambridge, Massachusetts to study art. She built up a reputation in Cambridge as an outrageous heiress with an unquenchable thirst for parties. The Cambridge high ended when one of her brothers, Minty, had a nervous breakdown, and was admitted to the same psychiatric hospital as Edie and committed suicide. The effects of his death drove Edie to leave Cambridge for New York where she lived with her grandmother and launched a modelling career.

Her epic shopping binges became notorious, as did her tendency to take parties of up to 20 people out for dinner. Patti would have daydreamed about Edie's super-rich lifestyle, where caviar and jewellery were habitual accessories.

Edie was petite, thin, vulnerable, fragile, beautiful and captivating. Her modelling career took off and soon she was one of the star models in *Vogue*. She travelled everywhere in limousines and ran up massive bills all over town that she was unable to pay. Edie's next tragedy was the death of another brother, Bobby, in a motorcycle crash. It was to be another catalyst in Edie's chaotic life which now included an increasing intake of drugs, especially speed and LSD, which she would gobble before going driving in her Mercedes. Patti recalls, in Jean Stein's book *Edie, An American Biography*, seeing Edie in *Vogue* in 1965 and how she immediately connected with the woman in the photographs, wanted to emulate her.

Edie's reputation soon led to an introduction to Andy Warhol, who was wowed by her beauty and charisma and immediately invited her to become one of his superstars. She appeared in his art movies: *Vinyl*, *Kitchen*, *Beauty Part 11*, *Lupe*, *Chelsea Girls* and several others, and circa 1965/1966 the couple were constantly in the media spotlight, sporting the same hairstyle. Warhol opened an exhibition of his work in Philadelphia and Patti later told Edie biographer Jean Stein that she was present, travelling to the show by train from New Jersey. She said she saw Edie and that she was so enamoured with her that she spoke of having a crush on her. Patti would also have been in awe of Edie's involvement with The Velvet Underground, who were playing constantly at The Factory. Before long, the media attention caused Edie to feel she was outgrowing the confines of Warhol's Factory and she became friendly with Bob Dylan, whose manager Albert Grossman persuaded her to enlist his services in finding a Hollywood acting role, maybe in a movie with

Dylan. The relationship soured when Dylan married, although *Blonde On Blonde* and especially 'Just Like A Woman' are rumoured to be about Edie. Shunned by now by the jealous Warhol crowd, her notoriously self destructive appetite for drugs was now her sole raison d'etre.

The next Patti parallel came when Edie moved into the Chelsea Hotel at the end of 1966 and became romantically involved with Bob Neuwirth. After Edie set fire to her room, she returned to her family's ranch in California and was sectioned to another psychiatric ward. Once she was released, she returned to New York where in a haze of every narcotic imaginable she began filming *Ciao Manhattan* and continued modelling. By the end of 1968 she was destroyed by drugs and spent the remaining years of her life back in California in and out of psychiatric hospitals. A sudden marriage did little to emotionally heal the damage done by the drugs and she died of a barbiturate overdose in November 1971, aged 28, having literally worn her body out. When Edie died, Patti heard the news from Neuwirth and immediately channelled her grief into the poem entitled *Edie Sedgwick (1943–1971)* which lamented the death of her idol. Edie's romantic live-fast-die-young lifestyle mirrored that of other Patti heroes and heroines such as Janis Joplin, Jim Morrison and Jimi Hendrix who had all also died at the age of 27.

'Poppies' is one of Patti Smith's finest songs, mixing a Doors-like band jam with layers of poetic narrative. There are five separate vocal tracks. Patti's husky, sensuous tones are a clear catalyst to her declaring the album a sexy record. One section refers to Edie Sedgwick's tendency to hoard drugs and possessions, while another refers to Patti's hearing on the radio that opium fields had been burned down in Guam. A third section filters a woman's self discovery through a select history of goddesses, namechecking Venus, Sheba and Salome. It is an awakening, a woman's journey. The opening splutters and snippets of conversation could be a fourth voice, that of Patti herself. The fifth and main narrative is centred round the myth of Edie Sedgwick and concerns the scoring of some drugs: which lead to an overdose. The multiple vocal tracks enable the re-creation of the victim's mental condition as Patti describes the medical treatment of the overdose victim, while the band maintains a hushed tension. In a split channel, a separate vocal track continues the repetitive drug-scoring theme that was heard earlier. The victim is laid out on the bed. The amazing production then bounces each vocal from speaker to speaker; if you listen intently on a pair of headphones, three vocal tracks can be heard. One begins the radio segment, one reverb-soaked track doubles up that segment and a spoken whispered third track continues the overdose story – presumably a commentary on Edie Sedgwick's famed appetite for drugs. The climax of the song brings backs the Sheba, Salome, Venus awakening story, just after the death of the overdose victim. The final line links the speech at the beginning with the end, reminding the listener that the song's multiple storylines are framed by the making of a record.

'Pissing In The River' also works on multiple levels, but with an overall mood of disquieted spirituality. It could be read as a straightforward love song, but it seems more probable, in light of Patti's endless search for God, that it is a message to God. Her earlier comment that the record contains messages to God seems to relate specifically to this song. One lyric in the song works a martyr/saint paradox; the common habit of seeing a sense of God as a goal and also as a restriction. The third overtone is overtly sexual. It could also be a companion lyric to 'Ain't It Strange's demand to God to make a move. It's a beautiful song, crafted over melancholic piano and passionate crescendos. The squealing lead guitar at the end is a blast of premium Lenny Kaye fretwork.

'Pumping (My Heart)' swaggers with a musical nod to Roxy Music, the Stones and the exploding punk rock scene. The song was supposedly the band's attempt to write a dance song, and was loosely based around a dance that Patti and Lenny Kaye had invented at a discotheque in Pigalle, Paris. The dance was anchored around boxing steps. Patti saw the adrenaline-blasting song as mimicking the steps and finesse of a boxer or dancer. Again, Lenny Kaye is blasting his guitar riffs like a garage rocker with nothing to lose.

The proto-new wave sounds of 'Kimberly' on *Horses* were taken one step further by Allen Lanier's co-authorship on 'Distant Fingers', yet another track that talks directly to God. The swirling music offers the perfect vehicle for Patti's otherwordly lyrics, which are addressed to a higher being. The chorus is the first sign that Patti was becoming disillusioned with her quest for a spiritual connection. Poetry, rock'n'roll, performing – nothing could satiate her hunger for a communication with God. Patti's repeated assertion that she, like any true artist, was in competition with God had led her to a point of restless self-exhaustion. She was, in effect, competing with herself and her intangible ideals. She introduced an early version of 'Distant Fingers' on the WBAI radio broadcast in May 1975 saying the song was about her childhood and how she didn't fit in and felt at odds with everyone and everything.

The title track is an avant-garde guitar-driven sprawling mess of atonal noise which must have caused a few eyebrows to raise at Arista's offices. The sleeve notes state that both parts are dedicated to Arthur Rimbaud (thus providing a concrete link to *Horses*) and sculptor Constantin Brancusi. Some fans would say that this song was the prototype for the grunge sound that would dominate rock 15 years later. 'Radio Ethiopia' opens with guitar feedback and a muddy guitar riff that could be Black Sabbath or even Seattle's Soundgarden. Plectrums slide up and down guitar strings, exaggerating the dissonance.

When Patti's vocals do appear, she sounds possessed, as if speaking in tongues, a result of her interest in the Tower of Babel. Tribal drums pound, droning backing vocals loom. The music could be the blueprint for future intelligent and groundbreaking listening like The Fall, Live Skull, Come, Swans, Sonic Youth, Hole, or even Girls Vs Boys. By the end of the Seventies, New York City would be buzzing with a scene called the No Wave, a bleak, arty post-New Wave movement, which featured such acts as Teenage Jesus and The Jerks, James Chance & The Contortions and DNA. These acts all played harsh, dissonant music, which must have in some way been influenced by the drones and chimes of 'Radio Ethiopia/Abyssinia'.

Patti's vocals are mixed low in both parts, turning her voice into an extra instrument. A few phrases are audible, one echoing her father's advice to not be a pawn in God's game and her own belief that, in order to produce pure art, she must cast aside the idea of God. It was also a sign of her frustration with failing to find a form of God that she could relate to and feel. Her search for God was again being portrayed as a jail of sorts. Around the six-minute mark, the track gradually starts to disintegrate. Lee Ranaldo agrees that the 'sound' is undeniably one that influenced Sonic Youth. "By the time Sonic Youth had started I believe that all three of us – Kim [Gordon], Thurston [Moore] and myself – had totally absorbed every note on her records. Coupled with everything else going on back then – New and No Wave, and the Velvets etc – sounds such as 'Radio Ethiopia/Abyssinia' were sort of second nature by the time we started out, our background language, if you will."

The two-minute finale 'Abyssinia' is the handful of ash after the fire. As harsh harmonics and guitar feedback squalls fade out, Patti and the band sound totally burned out. For a band following up a hugely successful debut album, the inclusion of this track was seen as either self-indulgence or a defiant punk rock gesture of independence. It was a harsh noise work-out that made The Sex Pistols sound even more like a Seventies rock band with childish lyrics. The Patti Smith Group were closer in spirit to the hippies than the punks, but this epic song paved the way for many post-punk bands. The unreleased bonus track, 'Chiklets', which Arista tacked onto the album for the box set *The Patti Smith Masters* in 1996, is a laid-back, keyboard-driven jam that could have fitted onto the posthumous *American Prayer* album by Jim Morrison and The Doors. The lyrics are a stream-of-consciousness ramble, and the song was no doubt left off the original album because of its vagueness.

The sleeve notes contain a wealth of information, including the statement 'Free Wayne Kramer' written on the back cover, under the band photograph. Wayne Kramer was a guitarist in the legendary Detroit band MC5 (along with Fred "Sonic" Smith) who are often cited alongside The Stooges as one of the original punk bands. At the time of *Radio Ethiopia*'s release he was serving a jail sentence, hence the credit on the record sleeve. Kramer was first touched and then surprised by the statement: "One day in jail a guy came up to me with a Patti Smith Group album that said 'Free Wayne Kramer' on it and the guy said 'Is that you?' And it kind of surprised me since I didn't know her and then after I was released I stopped by when she was playing a gig in Ann Arbor. I went to say 'Hi' to her and thank her for keeping my name in the public eye while I was away, and she kind of shined me on. It was like she didn't know who I was nor did she care who I was, which threw me. With the benefit of hindsight I can see that it [the credit] was Lenny Kaye's doing."

David Fricke hears a strong MC5 influence throughout the album, especially the title track which, he reckons, owed a big debt to MC5's live epic 'Black To Comm'. Wayne Kramer, however, sees no connection: "'Black To Comm' was almost a free jazz explosion and I didn't hear any free jazz exploding on *Radio Ethiopia*. 'Black To Comm' was a set-closing piece that started with a single droning chord and an almost pounding gospel rhythm. And it evolved into a totally textural piece that varied every night and evolved into something different. I know

Lenny Kaye was well aware of what we were doing in MC5 and I think Lenny, from what I've heard, exposed Patti to the MC5. He kind of schooled her on what we and a couple of other bands like The Stooges were doing." The question of how Patti came to hear MC5 was clarified much later in a 1995 interview where Patti confirmed that it was Kaye who introduced her to MC5 and that 'Black To Comm', in particular, inspired 'Radio Ethiopia'.

The universal acclaim that had been heaped onto *Horses* turned into a mixed bag of critical responses. Richard Meltzer's review for *Creem* concluded that it was a "good 'un". Charles Shaar Murray for *NME* damned it with faint praise, calling it, "Just another well-produced, competently played mid-Seventies rock and roll record." It's hard to think how a record with a 12-minute improvised noise rock work-out could be a described as a standard Seventies album, but that was the lukewarm conclusion in *NME*. *Rolling Stone* condemned it as "an interminable Sixties freakout". This was also the case for record sales – where *Horses* had galloped into the Top 50 LPs, *Radio Ethiopia* didn't even make it into the US Top 100 LPs.

Patti was frustrated that the influential critic Lester Bangs disliked the record and felt that his feelings reflected a general misunderstanding of the album. As she saw it, Bangs felt they sold out with *Radio Ethiopia*, that they had produced a heavy rock album aimed at the mainstream – when of course they hadn't. On top of that, the album was not as widely available in record shops as *Horses* because some retailers objected to the title 'Pissing In The River'. This naturally incensed Patti and rallied her contempt for censorship.

Patti was at her most productive though and regardless of critical and commercial disappointments, the band again toured and played some of their most invigorating shows to date. A return trip to Britain was met with scores of superlatives, the most triumphant moments occurring during their two-night stint at London's Hammersmith Odeon on October 22 and 23, supported by The Stranglers.

The shows presented a Patti who was increasingly comfortable with her sexuality and sex appeal, to the extent that critics and fans began talking about how sexy they found her. Fred Patterson commented in a piece he wrote for *Back Door Man* on her undeniable sexiness: "I love Patti Smith for her wonderful rebellion – rock'n'roll. She breaks all the rules. She's the youngest person over 30. She's not packagably pretty like the polythene, pubic haired blondes on television, but she's sexy. Really sexy." It didn't matter if the fans and critics were male or female, straight or gay, they fell for her undeniable and fully blossomed appeal.

D.D. Faye remembers falling under Patti's spell: "She was so in touch with her own sexuality. People don't often talk about Patti Smith as a sexually exciting person, but she is. Everybody was sexually in love with her whether they wanted to have sex with her or not, because she was so free with her libido. She had libidinous energy." Patti also explained to D.D. Faye, in *Back Door Man* in April 1976, that performing and sex were often linked, especially when the chemistry between band and audience is perfect: "Rock'n'roll is still so young. It's open territory. When I lost my virginity, it was totally painful. I haemorrhaged for a week, but from all that pain and blood has come years and years of floods of sensations, which has made me crave loss of virginity in everything. It made me wanna fuck everything. There are times onstage when me and the guys look exactly alike, like when I was talking to you just now and you looked just like me. It's so exciting when you hit that moment. That ray gun telepathy. You can do it between two people or with a lover. It's a very sexual thing but it can be done without actually having sex. That's what rock'n'roll always was, a substitute for sex. And sex in its highest form is telepathic. So when you get to the point where the performer and the audience surrender to each other and go through a complete act of trust, a complete telepathic performance, then everybody can come."

When the band returned from the tour, Patti's increasingly manic drive got her banned from the WNEW-FM radio station for using the word 'fuck' on air on November 29. In response to her subsequent banning by the station's company, Patti wrote a piece entitled 'You Can't Say "Fuck" In Radio Free America' which was printed in the *Yipster Times* in March 1977. Patti's disillusionment after this censorship incident was just one example of her growing frustration with those who wished to hold her back.

The Patti Smith Group played a week-long booking at the Bottom Line and Patti's stage presence was becoming unnervingly intense. The record had bombed, her relationship with Allen Lanier, while long-term, was tense due to his rumoured infidelities, and her creativity was running at a furious speed. In spite of her rocky five-year relationship with Lanier, she bought a small New York City apartment to share with him.

On January 23, 1977, they opened for Bob Seger & The Silver Bullet Band at the Curtis Hixen Hall in Tampa, Florida, where only a tragic fall could stop Patti's feverish energies. The band were playing 'Ain't It Strange', and had reached the middle breakdown where Patti invites God to make a move, challenges him to appear to her, to give a sign that he exists. Patti turned round in circles, spinning faster and faster until she was whirling about the stage. The more frenzied her dancing became, the harder the band played. The crescendo reached a point of no return and suddenly the performance of the song became a metaphor for Patti's life which had been spiralling out of control. In a moment that looked like provoked intervention, Patti's frantic dancing caused her to trip on one of the onstage sound monitors and to the band's shock, she hurtled 14 feet over the front of the stage, collapsing below like a rag doll. The band at first were terrified that she might have killed herself, but although she was in agonising pain, she was conscious.

Patti's 14-foot fall severely damaged her neck, and she was immediately taken to a hospital in Tampa. She had a large gash on her head, and doctors diagnosed two broken vertebrae. To most fans it was a tragic accident, stopping her in her tracks, but to Patti it was the move from God she had been waiting for. Constantly looking for messages and answers, for an artist obsessed with trying to communicate with God the accident was loaded with meaning. To most people, it was a fall which could have killed or paralysed her. To Patti, it was no coincidence that the accident had occurred while she was singing 'Ain't It Strange'. She was inciting God to make a move and He did, hurling her 14 feet over the edge of the stage. Her competition with God was over and she was no longer obliged to challenge him. Patti's focus would now return to her lifelong search for a means to communicate with God. Like Rimbaud, Patti had failed to exploit the common idea of a God through language. Rimbaud had realised that he had failed to make himself a god, then proceeded to renounce the art form in which he had gloriously failed. Patti had developed a manic belief in rock'n'roll as a form of religion and believed that she could be a three-chord prophet, spreading her ideas to the masses. Infuriated by the lack of a visible God, she had decided to follow in Rimbaud's footsteps and become her own god. Her superstition, combined with the impression that it wasn't working, invested the Tampa fall with meaning that only she could rationalise – specifically that God had been following her attempts to challenge him and had struck her back down to mortal status. After leaving the hospital in Tampa and returning to the apartment she'd recently bought in New York, she experienced disturbed vision and a partial paralysis in her legs. She was condemned to strict bed rest and regular physiotherapy to assist her recovery. She was also permanently in a neck support.

Fortunately for her artistic sanity, Patti had secured a book contract with C.P. Putnam's shortly before the fall. The deal had come about after much discussion and when they finally gave her a $5,000 advance it was perfect timing, for within a few weeks of Patti banking the money she was bedridden. The project editor, William Targ, had been introduced to the idea of publishing a work by Patti about 18 months before by Andreas Brown from Gotham Book Mart. The contract gave Patti a purpose: stuck in bed, she wrote feverishly and continuously, fuelled by the strength of her painkillers. The enforced rest turned out to be a period of self-review, where Patti was able to meditate on the commercial and critical failure of *Radio Ethiopia* and the runaway success of *Horses*.

The first change in her life was the termination of her relationship with her manager Jane Friedman who, after a disagreement, was replaced with a lawyer who would manage Patti's affairs and deal with all legal matters. The band, meanwhile, were all effectively unemployed and had to find temporary jobs – no doubt a shock after performing to thousands. Patti continued her physiotherapy while writing what would become her collection of poetry, *Babel*. Her insistence on recovering quickly was partly based on her own troubled financial situation, but also on that of the band members. A period of intensive therapy in March 1977 led Patti and band to make a plan to appear at CBGBs on Easter Sunday, at a show which would be billed as 'La Resurrection' concert. It would be subtitled 'Out Of Traction, Back In Action', a wry comment on Patti's neck brace.

The period of rest also reminded Patti of what she saw as her roots as a poet, and writing the poems of *Babel* re-alerted her to the power of the word on the page, something which had been overshadowed by her rock' n'roll success. The CBGBs show was packed out but a little restrained due to Patti's neck brace, and obviously lower-key than the self-destructively vigorous *Radio Ethiopia* shows. Fred Patterson was present at most of these shows. He recalls, "During the late spring of 1977 I visited with some friends in New York City, kids who were *Back Door Man* readers and who would remain good friends: Miriam Linna, James Marshall and Todd Abramson. I met the critic Lester Bangs at that time and also The Cramps (Miriam was their drummer then) and Lydia Lunch (Miriam's room-mate). The Patti Smith Group played a series of early-evening shows at CBGBs. They were sort of spring training shows for the band because Patti was recovering from her fall in Florida – she was in a neck brace. Backstage at one of the shows I was introduced to Fred 'Sonic' Smith. He seemed a bit glassy-eyed and all he could do was point at my T-shirt, which happened to feature the MC5."

The Tampa fall was a moment of boundary-setting: The Patti Smith Group had finally gone too far and had found a limit and now that had been done, there was an air of retreat to their collective vision. They played some more New York shows in June and July 1977, including several at CBGBs. Their immediate thoughts were focused on making another record, something that they had been discussing before Patti's fall, when they loosely referred to the next album's working title as *Rock 'N' Roll Nigger*. Now it was talked about as an album of and about resurrection.

The relationship between Patti and Andreas Brown of Gotham Book Mart continued in 1977 when she handed Brown a poem she had written entitled 'Ha!Ha!Houdini!' and asked him to publish it in some form. Andreas Brown explains: "She said, 'Here I just wrote this and I like it and I want you to publish it for me and surprise me.' And she gave me her poem 'Ha!Ha!Houdini!' which was, in my opinion at the time, just a wonderful poem. So I spent a lot of time plotting and planning something special to sort of surprise her and please her. I found a vintage photograph of Houdini all in locks and chains and I used that on the cover of the book and then I cut the picture in sections, scattering it through the text so that it would show like the portion across the middle of the picture showing his wrists all bound in chains and locks. And then another section of his feet all chained with locks and then the strip of his head. Then on the special edition of that particular book (and it was done in wrappers, it wasn't a hardcover book) I punched the right-hand margin completely through the book and we put a lock through it and you got a miniature lock with a key so you had to unlock the lock to open the book. And then presented it to her at some particular point in time, I don't remember what the occasion was, and I think it's one of her all-time favourites among her publications. It's also become quite a rare book now, difficult to find and copies sell for $150. And we've done a few ephemeral pieces from time to time since, a few broadsides (what we call miniature posters or flyers), in commemoration of the art exhibit or something. And once in a while she'd do a reading and want to do a flyer or something."

Patti's bed rest enabled her, as planned, to complete her manuscript for William Targ by autumn 1977. Then it was time to start work on the band's third album, *Easter*, which was largely composed of songs they had been playing for some time. 'We Three' dated back to the Rock'n'Rimbaud shows while 'Space Monkey' and 'Privilege (Set Me Free)' had been live favourites since the band had hit the road after *Horses*. The late 1976/ January 1977 tour had also seen the appearance of

'Rock'n'Roll Nigger' in the set, which was met with hearty applause. Work began on *Easter* at the Record Plant in New York with producer Jimmy Iovine, and it was clear from the start that this would be a solid rock album compared with *Radio Ethiopia*, which was a document of creative overdrive, inspiration and spontaneity. It was the first recording that the band had done in winter and the climate suited the air of chilly spiritual introspection that dominated the lyrics.

Fellow New Jersey star Bruce Springsteen was next door recording what would be his *Darkness On The Edge Of Town* album and, because Iovine knew him, a collaboration took place between him and Patti. It was no secret that after the failure of *Radio Ethiopia* and the quiet media spell following Patti's fall, Arista was keen to see the band's third album make a dent in the record charts. Recognising the potential in a song the band were recording, Iovine asked Springsteen to lend his pop sensibilities to 'Because The Night', which he took away and returned re-written as a pop rock nugget. Patti and band weren't entirely happy with the re-write, so she altered his lyrics. Later it would be widely perceived as a Springsteen-penned hit when in fact he had merely tightened the structure and simplified the lyric. The recording of the album was again workmanlike and, by the end of 1977, Patti's resurrection was ready to go with a book of poems and her most commercial album to date in production.

By the time *Babel* was published in February 1978, Patti had become romantically involved with Fred 'Sonic' Smith, a musician who had played guitar for MC5, Ascension, the Scott Morgan Group and fronted Sonic's

Rendezvous Band. The two had met on March 9, 1976 when Arista had thrown a party for her and the band in Detroit, a story she told Lisa Robinson in a piece that ran in *Interview* in 1988: 'We met in 1976 at the Lafayette Coney Island, a famous little hot-dog and chilli place in downtown Detroit. My record company had a party for me there. Fred and I met in front of a white radiator and the communication was instantaneous. It was more than that: it was mystical, really, something I never forgot. But I didn't see him again for almost a year."

In February 1978, Patti and Lenny Kaye made a brief trip to Los Angeles to take care of some business associated with the imminent release of *Easter*. The staff of *Back Door Man* heard that the couple were heading to LA and jumped on an opportunity to celebrate the third anniversary of the magazine's launch. Fred Patterson remembers how D.D. Faye persuaded Patti to play at their party: "On February 10, 1978, D.D. Faye got wind of Patti being in town with only Lenny Kaye. She was able to set up a *Back Door Man* Third Anniversary show at the Fleetwood in Redondo Beach. The plan was for the duo to perform some songs and read some poetry. Members of the band The Pop, who had played earlier, joined her for some songs. It was a gas." Patti read *Seventh Heaven* and she and Lenny hammered through renditions of 'Radio Ethiopia/Abyssinia' and 'Gloria'. They also celebrated the location of the party by opening their set with 'Redondo Beach'. Patti commented that it was the seventh anniversary of her musical union with Lenny. To celebrate the occasion, Lenny Kaye inscribed a book that D.D. Faye had with her, called *The Speed Freaks* by Peter L. Cave, with the following: 'Thanks for getting our 7th anniversary together, love Lenny K xxx." Patti also wrote on the book, choosing to scrawl her message across the first page which was blank except for the book's title: "Dee Dee, To the best since Marianne Faithfull, Patti Smith."

Babel showed off another collection of classic Patti poetry. Its format split the poems into seven different sections and each section was a mixture of black-and-white photographs and text. A dedication appeared at the end of the volume thanking Andi Ostrowe who had developed an even deeper friendship with Patti after her fall. He spent the majority of Patti's recuperative period sitting with her and playing nurse, confidante and scribe. Patti was often under the influence of powerful pain-killing drugs and sometimes the chemicals would re-activate the hallucinatory mind rambles that had occurred throughout her life. In these states, Patti would frantically spew out lines of poetry and Ostrowe would sit at a type-writer and struggle to note everything down on paper.

Babel also further blurred the line between rock'n'roll lyrics and poetry, with the inclusion of full or partial lyrics within the book. The spoken-word section to 'Poppies' crops up in the title poem, while 'Ain't It Strange', 'Space Monkey', 'Babelogue' and 'High On Rebellion' all appear as they do on record – cementing Patti's blurring of lyric as poem, poem as lyric. The homages to heroes and heroines continued with poems for Edie Sedgwick, film-makers Pier Paolo Pasolini and Robert Bresson, Georgia O'Keefe, Bob Dylan and Maria Falconetti. Patti was increasingly sensing that the qualities she looked for in these figures were close at hand and this was reflected in her poems for Fred Smith and Lenny Kaye.

The book inspired many of her fans, as much as her

music. For instance, Sonic Youth's Lee Ranaldo who said: "The records may be more significant culturally, but I carried *Babel* under my arm for about a year as though it were a sort of young person's key to the universe."

Babel was published in the UK by Virago Press, who ran the following across the front cover: "A tidal wave of dreams, hallucinations and ecstasy from the High Priestess of Rock." In spite of her fall and the subsequent period of recovery, Patti was now seen as 'the High Priestess Of Rock', a tag which the release of the remarkable *Easter* album would rubber-stamp.

6

Patti's Resurrection

THE *Easter* album was a multiple resurrection for Patti Smith. On a literal level, the record symbolised her rock'n'roll resurrection after her terrifying fall in Tampa. After almost a year of recuperation, she was returning with a new album. On a personal level, she was emotionally resurrected by her love for Fred Smith. Her documented struggle or competition with God was beginning to transform into a journey where she would become spiritually re-aligned with her idea of God, rather than having to compete with Him. The most obvious indication that her struggle to overthrow God from her life was over appears in her quotation from the Bible on the inner sleeve of *Easter*: "I have fought a good fight, I have finished my course" which is taken from 2 Timothy 4:7. The verse in the Bible continues: "Henceforth there is laid up for me a crown of righteousness, which the Lord, the righteous judge, shall give me at that day: and not to me only, but unto all them also that love his appearing." The traditional list of inner sleeve thank-you's also includes Fred 'Sonic' Smith. Patti was paving the way for the grand finale of *Wave* by dropping two subtle hints of what was to come.

The album cover was again used to express Patti's current state of mind. She had journeyed from the tomboy posturings of the *Horses* cover through the distant and distracted image of Judy Linn's *Radio Ethiopia* cover to arrive at this supreme statement of female power. The photograph was this time shot by Lynn Goldsmith, who had taken the band photograph that appeared on the back cover of *Radio Ethiopia*. It is an astonishing photograph, which captures the tension that lies at heart of the record's songs. The album is about Patti's discovery of her womanhood, the re-awakening of her spiritual relation-ship with a sense of God and her opening up to genuine love. The photograph speaks volumes: Patti poses in a defiant model's stance, hands playing with her hair. On the cover of *Radio Ethiopia*, one hand played with her hair in a tentative unsure manner, as if she wasn't comfortable with such a feminine gesture. The other hand was par-tially clenched, awkward and tense. One eye wasn't even visible, the other stared into space with a vulnerable gaze. Her hair was just past collar length, tucked behind her ear.

Most importantly, both *Horses* and *Radio Ethiopia* used a black-and-white photograph as the cover portrait. *Easter* remained the only Patti Smith album cover that is in full colour until the release of *Twelve*.

The album is a resurrection, a time of sorrow and joy, so what better than a sleeve shot that combines earthy browns (the soil of the grave) and soft flesh pinks (resur-rection and life). Patti still wears a ring on her left hand and a gold bracelet adorns her right wrist. Several neck-laces hang around her neck just as a solitary necklace is visible on the *Radio Ethiopia* cover – her gradual drift towards femininity is obvious in the move from a man's tie to a single necklace to several necklaces. Patti was, consciously or unconsciously, becoming a woman. The pose she strikes is defiant, assertive and, above all, strong. Gone is the vulnerable air of her previous album. The new resurrected Patti is pouting, eyes cast down, a mass of dark hair, eyebrows and eyelashes. Her back is slightly arched – not the body language of someone who is unsure of their identity.

The second most fascinating fact about the image is the amount of flesh on display. Patti had been mostly covered up before; now she was dressed as if she was halfway between bed and the streets. The most notorious part of this cover shot is of course the fact that she had visible armpit hair. It was a typically intelligent way to subvert the traditions of the female rock singer's image. Patti appears to be bowing to the female singer marketing clichés by revealing a stretch of inviting flesh, but then the parody of the image becomes clear. The armpit hair re-claims the right for a female singer to appear on her record sleeve in a pose that is sexual, erotic and powerful without compromising or debasing female dignity. Patti re-wrote the music industry rules yet again. The moronic reactions to the sight of a female armpit prompted debates in the US and the UK, whereas nobody even commented on it in Germany and France. The cover is the perfect symbol of the resurrected Patti Smith.

Robert Mapplethorpe's sleeve portraits (entitled *Patti: dark* and *Patti: light*) capture the split in Patti's self-image. The dark image has Patti blindfolded, dressed all in black and posing uncomfortably with arms outstretched. In direct contrast to the dark photograph's androgyny, the light image is extremely feminine, with Patti draped in what appears to be a gown made out of bed sheets. Her right side seems soft, her left side is tensed up, with her hand scrunching up the backdrop curtains. She also has her back to the camera, suggesting that she isn't totally comfortable with an outright feminine image. Neither is she at ease with the tomboy androgyny image. The cover of *Easter* brilliantly pinpoints the halfway point between both images, allowing Patti to be tough and masculine in air but also assertively female in body and spirit.

Easter was released in April 1978 and was a commercial success, chiefly due to the smash hit single 'Because The Night' which Bruce Springsteen had helped Patti to perfect, while they were both recording at the Record Plant. Patti re-wrote some of the lyrics, making it a specific love song to her lover Fred Smith, as she told *The Big 0* in 1995: 'The lyrics I wrote for Fred. We had fallen in love and it was intentionally like that. I was away from him and I was longing for him. It was written as a song for him and letting him know how much I wanted to be with him."

The single peaked at number five in the UK Top 40 singles chart and at number 13 in the US. The combination of Springsteen's ear for a conventional pop song and the simplistic classic rock'n'roll lyric was a sure-fire formula. The album itself made it to number 16 in the UK and to number 20 in the US. It is an album about rebirth, resurrection and transition. As D.D. Faye explains, "I thought *Easter* was as tortured as anything else she's done. I thought it was incredibly intense. The album's about death and longing. Starting something and ending something. The process of constant transformation, which is ultimately what Patti Smith is all about." Patti had found

her real lifelong love with Fred Smith, leaving her relationship with Allen Lanier behind. She was re-defining her
personal image and beginning the journey towards marriage and motherhood. The Springsteen collaboration
was a bid to take her specific sound to a wider audience, a
carrot to draw the masses to her vision. Her search for
God was starting to become an exercise in humility and
grace rather than a defiant challenge.

'Till Victory' is a jubilant cousin of 'Ask The Angels',
and a celebration of rock's possibilities as a subversive
weapon. Patti is again citing rock'n'roll as a weapon, the
electric guitar as a means of fighting for personal freedom.
'Space Monkey', which appears as a poem of the same
name in *Babel*, is difficult to comprehend, and is reminiscent of the fragmented writings of William S. Burroughs.
In *Babel* the verse is set around a picture of Tom Verlaine.
Musically, the song is quite similar to Verlaine's work
with Television. Patti offers a jumble of rambling images,
namely another UFO reference and the first of *Easter*'s
two references to cocaine, the other appearing on 'High
On Rebellion'. Allen Lanier and Richard Sohl both
appear on the song, contributing keyboards.

'Ghost Dance' was written quickly by Lenny Kaye,
and Patti took a cassette recording home and worked on
the lyrics. By the end of the evening, she and Lenny were
linked up by telephone working the song out. The result
was a slice of acoustic trance rock, which ended up almost
hypnotic because of its mood. The title referred to the
Native American Indian ritual of the ghost dance, which
was performed in a bid to communicate with the spirits of
those who were dead. Its supreme purpose was to attempt
to raise the physical presence of a dead spirit. This was

another song about different modes of communicating with God and parallel planes of existence. The song was to have a chilling emotional subtext when it was dusted off and played on the *Gone Again* tour, because of all those who had died around Patti.

Much scrutiny and critical glare were directed onto 'Rock'n'Roll Nigger', a song that attempted to declare the word nigger redundant as a racist slur and reclaim it as an outlaw tag for outcasts. As Patti often pointed out, the word nigger to her was a term for anyone living on the fringes of conventional society. Dave Marsh, reviewing *Easter* for *Rolling Stone*, was unsure if this was a wise and responsible artistic move, writing that the song was "an unpalatable chant because Smith doesn't understand the word's connotation, which is not outlawry but a particularly vicious kind of subjugation and humiliation that's antithetical to her motive". However, Patti had grown up in a black neighbourhood and only those acutely unfamiliar with her work could misconstrue her message.

The Doors-style breakdown after one minute has Patti voice a familiar train of thought among artists and visionaries, namely that when a person suffers, they are consequently invested with the wisdom to comprehend suffering. It is a recycling of the myth of the suffering artist, the Rimbaudian ideal of suffering for art. 'Babelogue''s live stream-of-consciousness sound turns from a frenzied babble to the guitar rifling of 'Rock'n'Roll Nigger'. After a yelp by Patti, Lenny Kaye sings a verse. The snarled lyric, revolutionary attempts at redefining language, and aggressive delivery suit the punk rock mood of the time perfectly.

'Privilege (Set Me Free)' was a cover of the title track

from the John Hayman and Peter Watkins 1967 movie *Privilege*, which starred Jean Shrimpton and Paul Jones. The movie satirises rock music by having Jones play a rock star who is controlled by the Government to manipulate fans. The message is that rock music is no longer the dangerous rebellious tool that it was when it began to become popular. New keyboardist Bruce Brody, who had temporarily replaced Richard Sohl, plays a church-organ introduction, lending the song a highly appropriate religious overtone, since Patti goes on to rap a slightly adapted version of the beginning and latter part of *Psalm 23*, a psalm of David.

The song made it to number 72 on the UK singles chart, where it was issued as an EP with a poetry reading on the flipside. Her cry at the end of the song was recycled by R.E.M. on their album *Life's Rich Pageant* when Michael Stipe shrieked the same words at the end of 'Just A Touch'.

'We Three' sounds like a slowed-down mature attempt at re-writing something by The Ronettes, with a sombre doo-wop piano line accompanying Patti's tale of a splintering ménage a trois. Patti's vocal performance is powerfully emotive, ranging from rich velvety tones to an exasperated rasp. The key change about two thirds of the way through raises the pitch and turns the piano line into something closer stylistically to honky-tonk. Fred Patterson, in his review of *Easter*, picked up on the song's melancholic tone: "The song has a sad, melancholy R&B feel, like 'These Foolish Things' by The Dominoes, 'Every Beat Of My Heart' by The Royals and 'Blue Velvet' by The Clovers. The song concerns a guy who loves a girl who loves another guy."

127

Seconds after the pretty end to 'We Three' comes the gritty Steppenwolf-heavy guitar fusion of '25th Floor' and 'High On Rebellion' (which also appeared in verse form in *Babel*). The combined parts make six minutes of punk rock, with Patti free-forming over the band, who sound like a collision between The Velvet Underground and 'Sympathy For The Devil' by The Rolling Stones. 'High On Rebellion' was the climactic section, with Patti improvising her poem about the powers of rock'n'roll and electric guitars. '25th Floor' wields a heavy Seventies rock riff and fragments of squealing lead guitar which wouldn't be out of place on a Led Zeppelin record. Bruce Brody's primitive synthesizer sweeps throughout, occasionally falling into pomp-rock territories. Patti's voice is gruff and rugged, recalling Janis Joplin. The spoken-word segment is thrust high in the mix, putting Patti's words over the band's Velvet Underground-esque jamming and Lenny Kaye's piercing and treble-soaked solo.

The closing title track is astonishing and takes Patti and her band far beyond the boundaries of what a rock song is or should be. The droning mournful organ, Jim Maxwell's bagpipes and the haunting chiming bells give the song its elevated spiritual mood. The sense of ascension and resurrection is captured by the music, whose trancelike quality fits perfectly with Patti's address.

The name Isabella being repeatedly sung throughout the song is explained in Patti's liner notes as being a reference to one of Rimbaud's sisters, Isabelle, whose first communion happened in July 1871 (the subject of Rimbaud's poem 'First Communion').

This spoken-word break is Patti's most extraordinary moment, combining a true poet's delivery and phrasing

with beautiful poetic images, which capture Christ's crucifixion and resurrection. Tranquillity and transcendence
come after the brutality and tragedy of the crucifixion.
After years of searching for God and the one true love that
would make her feel real, loved, whole and alive, and
after her Tampa fall, Patti's parched and dry voice offers
self-sacrifice and resurrection via art.

There was no question that, despite some of the songs
being from earlier eras, it was still a blinding album, and its
release in Easter 1978 cemented not only her personal
resurrection but her reputation as a major artist. The key
to its success was the superficial impression that it was
more commercial in sound than its predecessor.

When 'Because The Night' turned into a hit single, it
was good news for Patti that her audience was widening
but it was slightly disappointing for the band that their
lightest song to date should be their hit. Nonetheless, it
was a smash single which delighted the label – and critics
were fairly universal in their praise of *Easter*. The record
did introduce her to a wider audience.

As before, the band went on the road to play the songs
live, and in April 1978 The Patti Smith Group appeared
in the UK, playing two concerts at the Rainbow theatre
in London and one in Manchester. She was also interviewed for Granada TV and recorded another performance on the BBC's *Old Grey Whistle Test*, which was
broadcast on April 4. The band played 'Because The
Night' and '25th Floor'. The Rainbow appearances were
again characterised by a sprawling lengthy version of
'Radio Ethiopia/Abyssinia' which some fans and critics
rated as the worst part of each show.

The UK shows were followed by some brief European

dates which took in Berlin, where the audience were treated to a cover of The Kinks' 'You Really Got Me' and a full version of 'Land'. Another German show, in Essen, unveiled 'Revenge', covers of Manfred Mann's '5-4-3-2-1' and the Elvis Presley staple 'Jailhouse Rock'. A concert in Paris contained two unusual tracks: 'I Was Working Real Hard' and 'Keith Richards Blues' (a jam referring to his drug-bust problems in Canada).

After this, Patti and the band returned to the States for the US tour which ran throughout the summer of 1978. The tour saw Patti again returning to the manic fervour that had characterised her life before the fall, but this time she had an anchor in the growing love between her and Fred Smith.

In June the Robert Miller Gallery in New York opened its doors for Patti and Mapplethorpe's joint exhibition, an event that came about after Miller had seen her drawings at the Gotham Book Mart store gallery. Media coverage of the exhibit was high, and only added to the mass of Patti Smith coverage at the time. The US tour was followed by a triumphant return to the UK, to play at the 18th National Jazz Blues and Rock Festival in Reading, Berkshire (later known as the Reading Festival) on August 27. The band then crossed over to Ireland, to play in Dublin on September 3. After Ireland, they played in Dusseldorf, Bremen, Nuremburg, Berlin, Ludwigs-haven, Munich, Vienna and Brussels.

Poetry readings were fitted into the schedule alongside the rock concerts in support of Virago Press' edition of *Babel*. A reading in Edinburgh featured '25th Floor', 'dog dream', 'rape', 'edie sedgwick', 'dream of rimbaud', 'Girl trouble', 'Hunter Gets Captured By The Game', 'Sally',

'Neo Boy Parts 1&11', 'I was working real hard' and 'Prayer'. A reading in Dublin had a slightly different set: 'Broken Flag', 'Hunter Gets Captured By The Game', 'Poppies', 'Jenny', 'Gloria', 'Pinwheels', 'Thread', 'rape' and 'marianne faithfull'.

Once the dates were complete, the band returned to New York during the third week of September, and Patti made some important decisions. She had met her equal and ideal in Fred Smith and had attacked the British music press while on the UK tour for gossiping about her split from Lanier and love for Fred. This was just one incident in an era when Patti's dissatisfaction with the music industry was running high. She was tired of the press and aware that The Patti Smith Group had probably peaked as a unit. She was conscious that she wasn't as passionate as she had been and that she wasn't giving her entire being any more. Touring was also still hard because of persistent difficulties and pains from her Tampa fall. On returning to the States, Patti gave the first clear indication that she was thinking of giving her rock dreams up when she left her beloved New York City for Detroit. The reason for the move was quickly revealed to be Fred Smith, who had his roots there (he had begun his musician days there with MC5). Considering the number of times she had championed and credited New York City with changing her life and giving her a home, her move indicates not only that she wanted a change but also that she was deeply in love with Fred.

7

Wave Goodbye

PATTI spent the winter of 1978–1979 recording *Wave* with producer and long-time friend Todd Rundgren, who earned the band's respect by interfering only when they were stuck on where to place a song's bridge or chorus. He would also offer helpful advice on specific arrangements. Patti confided her plans to retire from her musical career once *Wave* was released and a farewell tour completed to Rundgren but not to the band. The members of the band had had their suspicions when Patti moved to Detroit, but since she hadn't mentioned anything, they just assumed they were being overanxious. Patti had reached a point in her life where she had been searching for some personal peace and she had finally found a degree of it, not in her poetry or music but in another person's love.

D.D. Faye sees Patti's lifelong search as a motivator: "Patti Smith's constant search is for resolution and the resolution for her is art. Whenever she produces any art, she is resolving elements. All these elements are at war with her, and sometimes they're not and they merge beautifully, and therefore it comes out as art. I always saw Patti as an expression of elements. I also think she's always been very comfortable with the idea of God. For her God is just another element." The record in progress would clarify Patti's return to an idea of God, her acceptance of her self and her art and her celebration of a great love.

The title *Wave* can be read, with hindsight, as a veiled goodbye to music and her fans. Fred Smith and Patti were so in love that the album opens with a love song called 'Frederick'. This was a forthright move by Patti, making it clear that she had found a love more important than her love of/for music. Fred Smith had become her muse. Her relationship had become her art. The album is dedicated to him.

The cover features another Mapplethorpe photograph, this time a radical departure from the image that graced *Horses*. Patti poses in a white gown against a white background, with a dove perched upon each hand. A tree is positioned to her left. The image is almost religious, with Patti's stare a mixture of shock and transfiguration. She looks stunned and surprised, as though the love that she was experiencing was blinding in its intensity. After the hiding of her eyes on the *Easter* cover, her gaze here is direct and wide-eyed. Her left hand is a half formed fist, a defensive post for the dove to rest upon. This gesture represents the work she has decided to do before abandoning her art form. The dove (symbolising peace) is drawn against her hand and its wings are drawn tight against its body, indicating that it isn't going anywhere. Her right hand, however, forms a partially complete wave, whose full span is restricted by the other dove, which is poised as if it is merely passing by and is preparing to flee at any moment. This gesture is a wave goodbye to her fans and critics and the dove symbolises her finding of love which brought her inner peace. Her white dress is a traditional symbol of peace and acts as an admission that she has called a truce in her creative wars.

The white dress is also a pointer to her forthcoming marriage to Fred. The imagery is, effectively, an open letter to her more perceptive fans. Her competition with God ended in Tampa and now her acceptance of God is complete. The image is entirely feminine: there is no evidence of upper-lip hair, armpit hair, a tomboy's posture or clothes, or androgyny. This is Patti Smith, a woman who is loved and loves – her pondering of gender issues is obsolete. The inner sleeve photographs are part of a series that begins with the cover. There is another wistful close-up of Patti staring at and holding one of the doves. Her visible eye seems nostalgic or sad, which ties in with one of the album's themes, namely that the finding of true love also introduces an element of self-sacrifice into the lovers' lives. Patti knows the price of this love: the end of her rock'n'roll career. The band photograph is one of the nicest taken of the band and Patti and Lenny appear with huge smiles on their faces, as each member of the band waves what would be a goodbye (although they didn't know this; only Patti did). In a fourth photograph, she strikes a loose appropriation of the crucifixion pose, her arms outstretched as she vanishes behind the tree. Her whole body, especially her face, oozes resignation and defeat: the search is over. For Patti, it was only in the dis-covery of real love that she felt like a woman.

For other people, it was still a great record – although it was becoming obvious that her passion was waning, or becoming distracted. David Fricke, looking back with hindsight, has this to say about the album: "You know

Wave was actually a record that took me a little bit longer to like than *Easter* or *Horses*. In fact I liked *Radio Ethiopia* a lot more immediately because I've always been a freak for Detroit noise, and to me the MC5 were a big influence on that record. In terms of *Wave* I don't think of it as a goodbye; it just seems sort of like a slowing down. She had reached a point where she could recapitulate everything she'd gotten to. Maybe *Wave* was a grand gesture or goodbye, but I didn't know it at the time."

Patti's growing disillusionment with rock music as a tool of expression was highlighted by her inclusion of the band's cover of 'So You Want To Be (A Rock'n'Roll Star)' by The Byrds: the sneering lyrics have been covered by many a disaffected artist. The artist who had celebrated music and all its legends now found herself artistically spent. Her mistrust and contempt for the press was well known. The dream had soured. The youthful energy and passions of *Horses* had given way to a bitterness that is obvious in the way that she sings this song. The rock'n'roll manifestos that were so plentiful in *Radio Ethiopia* and *Easter* had now faded, and she realised now that she had been drained by the music business, just as Jim Morrison, Jimi Hendrix and countless others had. She had no intention of becoming a rock martyr and, as she had already planned to abandon her rock career after a final tour, the inclusion of this song served as yet another explanation of her impending retirement.

In complete contrast is the fragility and humility that lie at the heart of 'Hymn', a gentle lullaby. Musically, it is an early companion piece to 'The Jackson Song' on *Dream Of Life*. It can be read literally as a hymn, in the deepest religious sense, as another attempt by Patti to communicate with God. The frustration of her earlier cries to God ('Ain't It Strange') now seem to have developed into a bond and understanding with her sense of a stronger God. On another note, it could be read as a wordplay game, with 'Hymn' really meaning 'him', making the song another love song written for Fred. It is Patti at her most transcendent, with possible allusions to childhood, God and love, the three topics that would shortly define who she was to become.

The song 'Dancing Barefoot' appears in most Patti fans' top five favourite songs. The sleeve notes dedicate 'Dancing Barefoot' to Jeanne Hébuterne, Modigliani's lover. The mostly sung, partly spoken vocal performance enhances what was becoming a clear Patti formula: perfectly joining poetic phrasings to intelligent rock lyrics. The crescendo of the song rises and surges, allowing Patti to break in with her intense spoken word piece. Mixed behind the spoken word vocal track is the sombre repetition of phrase which seems to say that falling in love is both a joy and a sacrifice – a form of submission: hence the Hébuterne succumbing to Modigliani dedication.

Jeanne Hébuterne (1898–1920) was a beautiful 19-year-old art student when she was introduced to Modigliani, who was then notorious among Parisian art lovers, but still poverty-stricken and regarded as a drunk. They became romantically involved almost immediately, which enraged her wealthy Catholic father because Modigliani was Jewish and by this time very poor. Her response was to move out of her parents' home and into a squalid hotel with Modigliani. By early 1918 they were living in the South of France to escape the shelling of Paris, and Hébuterne was pregnant. Their first daughter was named after Jeanne, who was pregnant again by the time they moved back to Paris. Modigliani never married Hébuterne, despite publicly referring to her as his wife, and when he died she was nine months pregnant. Her father took her back to the family house, where, consumed by grief, she threw herself and her unborn child out of a fifth-storey window, dying instantly. Her family refused a joint funeral and buried her at a private ceremony which was closed to her friends. Modigliani's family raised the orphaned daughter and after much pressure, persuaded the Hébuterne family to exhume Jeanne's remains, so that she could be re-buried with Modigliani in the Père-Lachaise cemetery in Paris. Hébuterne was the driving force behind Patti's fantasies of becoming an artist's mistress, and when Patti had first arrived in New York, she was determined to model her life on somebody like Hébuterne. Within the context of 'Dancing Barefoot', Hébuterne is mentioned in association with the great sacrifices that must be made in return for love. For Hébuterne it was her life, for Patti it was her music, her fame and her adopted home.

Critically, *Wave* was deemed her least successful record but commercially it was her biggest seller to date. After its release in May 1979, it peaked at number 41 in the UK album charts and number 18 on the US album charts, thus making it a commercial hit. The UK 7″ of 'Frederick' made number 63 on the singles chart.

In spite of the sales, there were two tracks that diluted the spiritual concerns and strength of the album: 'Seven Ways Of Going' and 'Citizen Ship'. 'Citizen Ship' is a heavy keyboards driven dirge, with Patti launching an assault on conformity and society's codes. Supposedly, the song chronicles a chain of events that all happened in 1968 and offers insight into the personality of her band; the fact that it isn't clear to the listener suggests that she had become too narrow in subject for her meaning to be translated. And 'Seven Ways Of Going' is a sombre, psychedelic bluesy jam, complete with squealing saxophone and strangled guitars. The lyrics are again difficult to comprehend. The song also dates back to 1974–75 when Patti would perform the chorus hook unaccompanied and spin tales and poems in between.

Far more personal is the classic Seventies rock of 'Revenge' which packs a hammer heavy chorus. Lyrically, it's a big kiss-off to an ex-lover. The ex-lover never cared like she did, never paid much attention to their love and now she's taking great pleasure in getting even. It's a standard 'you done me wrong' break-up song.

'Broken Flag' is credited on the liner notes as being about Barbara Frietchie, who in 1862 defiantly waved the Union flag in the face of the oncoming enemy as they approached Frederick, Maryland. The mournful anthemic music washes over Patti's deeply emotional vocals. It is a song of self-sacrifice, another comment on her public sacrifice for the love she believed in. It is another coded explanation of why she will give up her art in the name of love. It is a dream of love she has found with Fred and, despite the sacrifices she will make, she cannot resist the dream. And like Barbara Frietchie, Patti is prepared to lay down her creative public life for someone or something that she believes in.

The final song is aptly entitled 'Wave' and is an eerie address to the Pope Albino Luciani. Over ghostly piano Patti half-speaks, half-whispers. It is like an open prayer or a letter and underscores how far she had come on her spiritual journey. The Patti who sings 'Hymn' is reconciled with God, after years of being in competition with Him and then in search of Him. The central subject is the Pope, waving from the Vatican, but as in most of Patti's songs, there is a buried dialogue at work between her and God. Abstract phrases sit alongside what seems to be part of a conversation. Sometimes the song can conjure up the image of a solitary figure walking along a beach, waves lapping at their feet. At other times it seems otherworldly, as if it's acutely spiritual. It also serves as a goodbye to her music fans. The touches of cello and atmospheric sounds are perfect in their subtlety: the ghostliness of the track is a tribute to Todd Rundgren's production work. The end of the track is the end of the first chapter of Patti's musical career: this is self-explanatory.

Wave is an astonishing gift of love to Fred Smith. The album is dedicated to him, the opening song is for and about him. The tree on the record sleeve that partly protects her is, from an observer's eyes, a symbol for and of Fred's love for her. The track 'Wave' is a goodbye to her public life, because it becomes apparent that she no longer needs to search for love and approval through her art, she has found it on the private/personal level. It is also a document of her re-alignment with God, disguised on the album as the Pope.

The Patti Smith backlash in the press, which had been gaining momentum for some time, now reached an all-time high, with generally poor reviews of *Wave* appearing in most titles. *Rolling Stone*'s review said: "Though a long way from being a total disaster, *Wave* is too confused and hermetically smug to be much more than an interesting failure." *NME* savaged it. The critics in general felt that the record was lacklustre, lacking any genuine passion, and some attacked the first single 'Frederick' as little more than a re-write of 'Because The Night'. They overlooked the fact that, given Patti and Lenny Kaye's rock writer backgrounds, it made perfect sense that they'd want to write the occasional flat out pop song, and, as every critic knows, a good pop song instantly reminds you of another song. Patti's dislike of the press had reached breaking point, a fact that became obvious when she refused to grant more than a select few interviews for the album's release. The lucky few had to be screened by Lenny Kaye. He had to determine whether their motives seemed pure enough and their interest genuine enough for them to get an interview.

The Patti Smith Group headed out on a five-month tour from May to September 1979. Patti hated it. On the US leg of the tour she was visibly unhappy and would clearly rather have been elsewhere, namely with Fred. Her health began to give way. She told *Interview* in 1988: "I had bronchitis continually. It's a very unhealthy, self-involved life. I became extremely temperamental." Reports of just how temperamental and unhappy she was becoming appeared in a variety of publications. Her fatigue and ill-health became topics that she complained about both on and offstage. However, David Fricke claims that he saw some of her best shows on that tour: "Some of the shows she was giving on that tour were amazing. I saw her here at the Palladium and she played for two hours, and it was just everything she had ever wanted to do. She came out and played the clarinet, she read poetry, she rocked out on old Sixties British Invasion nuggets."

Patti and band played two benefit concerts for the Detroit Symphony Orchestra on May 17 at the University Of Michigan and on May 18 at the Punch And Judy Theatre in Grosse Pointe. Fred Smith's Sonic's Rendez-vous Band opened for both shows. The pair of shows raised $6,000 for the orchestra. These two dates were a rare moment on the tour when Patti was happy – because she and Fred were together. By the time the tour had reached Europe by the latter half of the summer, the sets included Dylan's 'Mr Tambourine Man' as well as the same set of covers that had been played on the *Easter* tour. Everything had become chaotic and stale and Patti was still deeply unhappy. To add to the pressures, crowd capacities had rocketed to sizes such as 30,000 and upwards. The US shows had seen her unable to make it through the opening line of 'Gloria' without breaking down, until, after too many episodes like this, it was removed from the set list. Often, she would dumbfound the audience by playing clarinet. The shows were tailored to the venue's size, meaning that 'Radio Ethiopia' was not played because its length would affect the crowd's rollercoaster ride of entertainment. Her London show at Wembley Arena on September 5 was met with hostile reviews rather than the blanket enthusiasm that had greeted her earlier London performances. *Melody Maker*'s Chris Bohn wrote: "Patti has a vision which became for her an obsession and our nightmare . . . This was not meant to be a crucifixion." The review's heading was "A Dream That's Over" and it went on to refer to the dullness of the concert. *NME*'s review ran under the headline: "So You Wanna Be A Rock And Roll Scumbag" and said: "I'm not knocking or gloating that she has softened, but I never expected it."

At the same time as these reviews were published, Patti Smith and band played the last of a series of concerts in Italy. The shows were so huge that there had been varying minor problems with crowd control. The final show was to 70,000 people in Florence, on September 10, 1979. The most telling moment of the entire show was when they put 'Gloria' back on the set list for a final performance. Patti altered the notorious first line so it instead stated that Jesus had suffered and died for her sins, in particular.

The closest insight into the Patti Smith who was in Florence can be found in her poem 'florence' which appeared in W W Norton's 1994 collection *Early Work*. It offers insight into the chaos of the Italian concerts, with memories of soldiers watching over the arena in Bologna and of her brother Todd managing the road crew. The rock'n'roll dream had soured and now the concerts were so large that any intimacy was impossible. The poem explains her awareness that the commitment and passion had gone. Patti was now distanced from her audience; she didn't want to get closer to them, she wanted to get closer only to Fred Smith, whom she desperately missed. The fans who she had once sought to preach to and entertain were now a mass of unfamiliar faces. Patti's love for Fred was growing so strong that she missed him to the extent that being onstage felt like a mere act for her. She wasn't giving herself fully, and she felt false being onstage and wishing she was back in Detroit.

Once the show was over, the band returned to the hotel, where Patti called them together and explained that she was no longer interested in playing music. She was exhausted, she was constantly unwell, she missed Fred, the shows had gotten too big, the passion was gone, they had done all they could do, the critics and press incensed her, she had found her one true love like a fairy tale and would put nothing before it. All of these factors led to her decision. The band were shocked. Her decision can't have been easy because of the number of lives she would affect by her decision. Her brother Todd was the road-crew manager. Her collaborator on *Babel*, Andi Ostrowe, was stage manager and tambourine player. And then there were obviously the members of the band. It was also devastating news for Arista, which had nurtured the band to stadium size only to see them split up. Patti's search was over, she had found what she wanted and was giving up her rock'n'roll dream to live with Fred Smith in Detroit.

In many ways, it was a logical salute to her heroes. Arthur Rimbaud had attempted to change the world and usurp the need for God through words and had (as far as he was concerned) failed. Once he realised that he was a mortal human being, the injury to his artistic pride forced him to admit defeat and to renounce all literature. His myth has been preserved by the secrecy in which he shrouded the rest of his life; and, to Patti, there could be nothing more romantic than writing a body of astonishing work and then abandoning literature. It is a move in keeping with the romantic tragic poet myth.

Jean Genet had been an outsider for all of his life – a homosexual, a thief, an orphan, an abandoned child and a convict – but, as critics have often asserted, he wrote his way out of a life sentence. His life imprisonment was rescinded only after Jean Cocteau insisted that Genet was one of France's greatest writers. Genet had documented his outsider's life in his novels and instead of further enforcing his distance from society, the novels in fact publicised his poet-thief myth. Consequently, his writing did the one thing he had contempt for: it acted as a passport to society, and upon realising this, he couldn't write another novel. Patti had spent her whole life painting herself as an outsider from society, a 'nigger', an artist. The reason she was an artist was because she felt she didn't belong to conventional society. She had worn an eye patch as a child, she had been thin and gangly, she was from a poor background and she had lost her art teaching scholarship due to a pregnancy. Patti saw herself as a genuine misfit who discovered acceptance only through abstract role models. She was hungry for approval and guidance and she found it in the writings of Arthur Rimbaud. Art gave her approval, fantasies and dreams; the artists became her teachers and friends. She didn't become an artist to achieve fame, fans, champagne and fortune; she became an artist in order to escape her inevitable lower-class future and to seek adventure. Patti's teenage years weren't spent chasing boys; they were spent in dreams where she was seduced by Rimbaud in Charleville, France, or was the tragic ill-fated Jeanne Hébuterne, throwing herself from a window because her beloved Modigliani had died. Patti wanted Paris or New York, she didn't want Pitman, New Jersey. In the same way, she was initially thrilled and shocked by the response to her poetry.

When Andreas Brown offered to publish her collection of poems, *Witt*, she was numb with joy. Her initial success as a poet was purer than her success as a rock'n'roller and when she began her manic quest for fame, it was as if Rimbaud and Genet had been knocked off her top ten influence list and replaced by simple rock-star icons like Mick Jagger and Janis Joplin. The Tampa fall stamped on her creative brakes and the writing of *Babel* re-opened her to the reality of her artistic vision. She had given herself to rock'n'roll, only to find that she was weaker than she thought. The adulation and the music industry machine had come close to chewing her up and destroying her, just as it nearly destroyed Bob Dylan. Her spell of recovery from the fall served as a time to re-think, just as Dylan's motorcycle accident had. A return to writing refocused her attention on her origin as a poet.

Patti had returned with a spiritual album that just happened to spawn a hit single. 'Because The Night' was a pop song in the truest sense: it was designed for mass popular consumption and the sales fulfilled this aim. The recognition and expansion of Patti's fan base was initially what she, her band and her record label wanted, but as soon as she realised that she was no longer a cult artist like Rimbaud but instead a rock star with a poetry reputation, like Jim Morrison, she jumped back, unsure of the monster she had created. Her fame drew her superficially into mass acceptance and, ultimately, society, making her albums a passport to belonging and fitting in, in the same way that Jean Genet's novels had superficially cancelled his outsider status. But, actually, she felt more alone and isolated than ever and her dissatisfaction fell awkwardly against the fact that now she was a rock star. She realised that it was something that she had never wanted on this scale. So she looked for a way out of her rock'n'roll fame, just as she had looked for a way out of her New Jersey youth. She found an escape route in the form of Fred Smith. She then staged a coded series of recorded and performed goodbyes and emulated Rimbaud and Genet by seemingly abandoning a phenomenal talent and art form.

Lee Ranaldo was unsure whether Rimbaud and Genet were behind her retirement, when he told me, 'While I certainly believe Patti to be well versed in the legends of these two famous literary raconteurs, I had never really thought about her 'retirement' in any such terms. It seemed to me that she had lived the rock life to the hilt, from poetess alone to duos with Lenny Kaye, and then the ultimate garage band backing her up, clarinet or hash pipe in hand (there's a picture of her toking on a pipe in *Babel* that always made an impression on me, as to her inner life of free-associative right-on visions, herb-inspired or not). I assumed that meeting Fred opened up the possibilities of other lives within her, those of family and motherhood and private poet. As for many other visionary artists, a change in mid-stream was for her, perhaps, a way out of the repetition of already won glories, the music bizniz game, and a chance for new experiences rather than the same old thing (even if that was amazing music!). The notion of a new life taking precedence over any status quo commitment."

While Ranaldo is definitely right, we can also see that Rimbaud had essentially freed her from New Jersey and, once free and in New York, she dedicated her first poetry-reading to Jean Genet. Their influence had always been strong, practically parental, and now it was time to stage her most theatrical and perplexing tribute to their legacies by renouncing rock'n'roll for a fiercely secret marriage in the suburbs of Detroit.

8

Wife, Mother, And Writer

ONCE Patti had officially left the band, she fled to her new life in Detroit with Fred Smith. The remaining months of 1979 were spent recuperating. Patti's health gradually regained balance and her frayed mental state stabilised. Fans and critics were puzzled by her retirement and some saw it as the direct result of Fred's influence; others fabricated rumours that centred on a mythical drug problem that had taken her to the point of collapse. Patti began the new decade by marrying Fred Smith, a natural step considering she had left both rock'n'roll and New York City to be with him.

The pair married on March 1, 1980 at a private cere- mony in Detroit attended only by both sets of parents. D.D. Faye and the staff of *Back Door Man* magazine were excited when they heard news of the wedding: "It was really nice that she didn't have to change her name, because although she's a real traditionalist, she's also very free. So it was good that she didn't have to face that dilemma . . . which is probably why she married him! It seemed obvious to me that she would marry Fred Smith; we just thought 'Why wouldn't she?'"

Fred Patterson has his own take on the subject:

"Although I know it pissed off a lot of people and let down certain other people, I didn't blame her for settling down with Fred 'Sonic' Smith in Detroit. I always felt that she had a right to her own life. We all do. Anyway, to me, she had done more for rock'n'roll in five years than anyone should expect."

Fred Smith was the perfect husband for Patti. They had a similar lower-class upbringing in common and were both notorious for their rock careers. Fred Smith had been the rhythm guitarist for Detroit proto-punk combo MC5, before going on to play for Ascension and the Scott Morgan Group during 1974/75. In 1976 he formed his own outfit Sonic's Rendezvous Band, along with Scott Morgan, bassist Gary Rasmussen and ex-Stooges drummer Scott Asheton. The Detroit 'supergroup' opened for Iggy Pop on his 1978 summer European tour because Fred was playing guitar in Iggy's band.

Fred Smith had been in bands from his early teens before joining MC5. To understand and contextualise the history and legacy of the band, I asked the other guitarist in MC5, Wayne Kramer, to elaborate on their story. He says, "We met in junior school in a neighbourhood called Lincoln Park in Detroit. A kind of working-class down-river suburb. All our parents worked in jobs related to the auto-industry . . . Fred's dad was a truck driver, my dad worked in an oil refinery, another dad was an electrician. I had a vision for a band so I looked around school for other people who wanted to be musicians too. We found a unity of purpose and really worked hard on getting that band together. It kind of came of age with the birth of the counter-culture. We were just ahead of the curve there and the growing sense of frustration with the slow pace of change and it kind of fitted in with our agenda, and the growing militancy among alienated white kids. And the anti-war, anti-oppression, anti-racist sentiment that was building."

MC5 started out as a band playing popular cover versions around 1964–65. Kramer recalls: 'We played songs we heard on the radio and later when Rob Tyner joined the band, he started turning us onto the blues and we started learning more rhythm and blues stuff. We played Motown tunes. We played a lot of jobs where we played five shows a night, seven nights a week, and you have to come up with a lot of songs to fill those nights. We kind of did our apprenticeship in the bars of Detroit and a lot of teen clubs and high school dances. Really, anywhere that we could play, we were there."

Prior to the official naming of MC5, they were all in other bands. Wayne Kramer says, "We were all parts of other rival neighbourhood rock'n'roll bands. I called one of my bands The Impressions; I had another one called The Bounty Hunters. Fred had a band . . . The Emeralds or something like that. And then Fred and I joined together and we called our band The Majesties and then finally when we got with Rob Tyner, Rob came up with the name MC5 because it sounded like a part number or a serial number or something, which was very Detroit-sounding."

The core of the band was established by the end of 1965 with the line-up of Rob Tyner (vocals), Wayne Kramer (guitar), Fred Smith (guitar), Michael Davis (bass), and Dennis Thompson (drums). In early 1967, John Sinclair became their manager. He was a radical thinker and writer who quickly fitted his political views to their rock'n'roll power. Soon they were gathering a reputation for raucous covers, heavy guitar originals and the political militancy of Sinclair's Trans-Love Energies group. When they signed to Elektra Records in 1968, they were drawing crowds of several thousand in Detroit. Kramer says, "We became enormously popular in the Detroit area and then in 1968 or 69 we signed to Elektra Records."

Elektra released the debut album, *Kick Out The Jams*, in the spring of 1969, but trouble sprang up between label and band over the appearance of the phrase 'motherfuckers!' on the title track. The band felt they had complete control but eventually the label ordered the censoring of the lyric. Kramer explains, "Elektra dropped us for unprofessional conduct while we had a chart-topping album. The album was in the thirties on the *Billboard* charts and the single was number two in Detroit and everything was going great guns. We were pretty committed to our ideas and we were told that we had complete artistic control, so we ran into some major conflicts with Elektra on the issues of control. They dropped us and Atlantic signed us and we did two more albums with them, *Back In The USA* in 1970 and *High Time* in 1971. Of the three, *High Time* is the best MC5 album. It was the most fully realised, it was a point where we had learned to make records. We could combine the energy of the MC5 live performance with the brainpower and the creativity that the band ultimately developed in the recording studio."

MC5 found that many radical fans regarded *Back In The USA*, which was produced by rock critic and future Bruce Springsteen manager Jon Landau, as a weakening of the band's vision and a betrayal of the sound of their free-jazz epic 'Black To Comm', which had dominated their live shows in the same way that Patti's shows from 1976–1978 were hinged on the improvisation of 'Radio Ethiopia'. By the time *High Time* was released, the band's popularity was fading, and on New Year's Day 1972 they played their final show together. Kramer saw their end as an inevitable consequence of their reputation for challenging their record labels and the way major labels tend to operate. He tells me, "The MC5 zeitgeist came and went and there was a change in the air and Atlantic Records had new bands like The Allman Brothers who were safe and they'd show up and just want to boogie, whereas the MC5 wanted to change the world through rock'n'roll. After a while the MC5 hadn't sold millions of records or hit that commercial mainstream vein and we were dropped, as simple as that. I was only 24 years old at this point and every member of the band's early adult life had been tied up in this project and all of a sudden it's all gone, turned to shit. It was a very stressful, depressing time and that's when musicians generally discover vodka and heroin in a major way." MC5's break-up in 1972 was symptomatic of their alienation. "We had no support from any other factions in the record industry and, after all, you're in a band to make records and be able to work and continue to develop and grow, and without a record company or manager, we really couldn't overcome the economic forces around us. The centre never holds. I can look at it now and trace a line from the shiny enthusiasm of the Sixties that built into the band's huge local following – when we were drawing 3,000 kids a night before we even put out an album, moving onto the peak of touring nationally and internationally – and then to watch everything start to fall apart and come down the other side. It's a textbook example of burning bright, burning hot and burning out."

Patti and Fred settled down in the Detroit suburb of St Clair Shores, where Patti was relieved to be out of the glare of the music press. Her personality was far more conventional and traditional than her image dictated and settling down and getting married was a source of enormous stability and happiness for her. Her constant search for something elusive didn't stop, but it was at least tempered by the love she'd always wanted. Fred could also understand what she had been through and judging from Wayne Kramer's story, he had ridden the same circus and ended up back at the bottom. Patti had quit the spotlight while she was at the very peak of her popularity and fame. Her last ever show was to 70,000 people and it might be that, having heard Fred's tales of life once the spotlight dies out, Patti decided to quit while she was on top. Her retirement was also unusual in that it afforded her the opportunity to disappear like her heroes and heroines (Jim Morrison, Jimi Hendrix, Brian Jones, Janis Joplin) had done, at the height of her fame, without actually dying. She effectively froze her legend in time.

The Patti Smith Group performed one final concert in June 1980 at Detroit's Masonic Temple. It was another benefit show for Detroit's Symphonic Orchestra. Patti began by reading some poems and then baffled her audience by reading Chapter 28 from the Gospel according to St Matthew from the New Testament of the Bible. The chapter deals with the resurrection of Jesus Christ and his subsequent appearance before the disciples. He instructs them to continue following his teachings and then disappears. It seems disturbing to imagine that Patti was comparing herself to Christ, but considering the extent to which she felt the music press were attacking (or crucifying) her and the extent to which the pressures of fame had got to her, it does fit. It is possible that Patti had finally reached a point where she had only one role model left: Jesus Christ. The more troubling fact is that Patti was born in December 1946, so that when she played this show she was thirty-three, the age that the Gospel, according to St Luke, reports Jesus' age to have been when he was crucified. Aware of this or not, Patti had undoubtedly developed some sort of Messiah complex. Her retirement in Florence acted as a metaphorical death and the concert in Detroit continues the comparison by having her resurrect herself for one final reminder of what her message was, just as the story of Christ's resurrection did. The rest of the show featured 'Hymn' and two new songs, 'Torches' and 'Afghanistan'. There were also some covers and a piece where Fred played saxophone and Patti played clarinet. The new songs were never to be developed, as the resurrection show proved to be the last time she was seen in concert for a decade.

Much theorising has centred on Patti's so-called retirement; although it certainly seemed to be a fitting label for her disappearance, Patti views it quite differently. In many ways, the early Eighties were a period of development and growth for her. She was coming around from 12 hectic years in New York City. Initially, she found it incredibly difficult to leave her adopted city and felt isolated and lonely in Detroit, but she had never been a person who dwells interminably on the past, and she soon rose to the new challenge of settling down in her new home. She and Fred were both relieved to be out of the spotlight and keen to start a family. They were also keen to create art; not for the world, but for themselves. This type of art, they viewed as pure art. Neither of them had anything to prove outside their home. Fred's Detroit supergroup Sonic's Rendezvous Band had disbanded in spite of much local acclaim, leaving their fans only one recording, a 7″ single entitled 'City Slang'.

Patti took one further step towards improving her health. She decided to stop smoking marijuana. Her decision was explained to the *Philadelphia City Paper* in late 1995, where she told them, "I balanced myself in the early Eighties, slow in coming but very rewarding. I had never been much of a drug taker but I did smoke a lot of marijuana. I gave that up and was drug-free, which required a lot of concentration." Patti would now have a clear mind, enabling her to set about studying and writing – two pastimes which would dominate the Eighties.

Patti and Fred's first child was born in 1983, a son called Jackson. Patti was 36 at this point and had been anxious to start a family. Motherhood turned out to be a huge lesson for her, teaching her that the world doesn't revolve around the individual but instead around its people. The demands of motherhood took her away from the trappings of ego that most artists suffer and anchored her to a new outlook on the meaning of life. Her life was re-written by the demands of having a child. Routines and habits had to be reviewed and re-established. Patti's writing habits were also to change as she found herself having to write around the demands of an infant. This meant rising at 5am and writing for an hour or two before Jackson woke up. Music was still important and

Patti continued her clarinet playing, often with Fred at the piano.

Meanwhile, Lenny Kaye was still making music, this time with his own band, called The Lenny Kaye Connection, who put out a record in 1984 entitled *I've Got A Right* on the Giorno Poetry Systems label. It paid homage to his love of garage rock and ability to spot a pop gem, and even included a rock country ballad, 'Luke The Drifter', an early taste of his forthcoming infatuation with country legend Waylon Jennings. By the end of the Eighties, Kaye was working on a definitive Waylon Jennings biography which was published in the Nineties. The rest of his time was devoted to his increasing popularity as a record producer, which was first put under the critical spotlight when he co-produced the debut album by the then unknown New York female singer-songwriter Suzanne Vega. The eponymously titled debut album was a huge success (recalling the rise of Patti), largely due to her intelligent arrangements, soft voice and strong songs like 'Small Blue Thing' and 'Marlene On The Wall'.

His second major success as a producer was the stark but immaculately recorded solo acoustic album *Hips And Makers* by Kristin Hersh, who usually fronted Throwing Muses, a band who have always collectively acknowledged a debt to Patti's legacy and myth. He also produced Minneapolis band Soul Asylum's *Hangtime* album in 1988, as well as dozens of lesser known New York bands. In general, the Eighties saw Kaye's reputation grow as a music fan and all-rounder. He had worked in record stores, played guitar for Patti Smith, freelanced as a rock critic, compiled the epic *Nuggets* series of classic garage rock anthems such as Count Five's 'Psychotic Reaction', became known as a record producer, fronted his own band, dazzled everyone with his encyclopaedic knowledge of rock'n'roll and had even squeezed in a degree in American History before entering into a life in rock'n'roll.

The retirement period enabled Patti and Fred to mature as individuals. They'd done all the touring and lived out the high jinks of the rock'n'roll life and now they were both contented thirty-something parents. Patti spent more time at home than she had in New York, chiefly due to the transport system in Detroit. She had never learned to drive, and after her Tampa fall, she'd had recurring eye trouble which made her medically unable to drive, so she was dependent on Fred for transport. The couple watched over their child and settled into a regime of learning and re-evaluation. Patti studied 16th century Japanese literature and resumed her long-abandoned art studies, in particular drawing. Primarily she wrote a minimum of a quarter of a page each day. This period of growth continued until 1985 when Fred and Patti began working on some songs that they felt could turn into a new album. Once they were sure they wanted to make a record, rumours started flying that Patti was planning a comeback album. Nobody was sure if it was more than a mere rumour but speculation mounted.

The other major Patti Smith industry that had been working overtime during the Eighties was the legend business. She had been canonised as a High Priestess of Punk, a tag she had never felt drawn to, but her fans had not forgotten her and a small proportion of these fans had started their own bands under her spell. The imitators and successors were omnipresent. Fred was also aware that Patti's legend status could do with re-fuelling and they set about turning their home collaborations into an album.

There was much discourse about what Patti's 'comeback' album would sound like. After her sabbatical, nobody was sure how changed Patti's vision would be. Clearly, the perverse creative self-destructiveness of Rimbaud or Genet did not suit her situation and she was driven back to the public eye, less out of artistic necessity than, perhaps, a basic need to make a living. She was after all married and had a family and that brought financial responsibilities. The 'comeback' record had been expected for some time. Patti and Fred had always maintained an active commitment to writing and playing music, although initial talk about making a record had been silenced by the birth of Jackson. The next step was to invite original keyboardist Richard Sohl out to Detroit to work on new material. Once that was done, they started work in a studio only to discover shortly after beginning that Patti, now forty years old, was pregnant with their second child, who would be called Jesse. The record was delayed for another year. While Patti was pregnant, Fred continued working on and developing the album's songs, as well as lining up potential musicians such as ex-Sonic's Rendezvous bassist Gary Rasmussen to replace Ivan Kral.

Once Jesse was born and life was back to normal, the delayed recording sessions began at the Hit Factory in New York City in spring 1987, with Jimmy Iovine and Fred Smith sharing production duties. Scott Litt, who would go on to produce R.E.M., The Replacements and remix Nirvana, was associate producer. Richard Sohl was back on keyboards and Jay Dee Daugherty resumed his place at the drum stool. Ivan Kral had returned to his native Czechoslovakia and was replaced on bass by three different bassists: Gary Rasmussen, Kasim Sultan and Bob Glaub. Guitar duties were handled by Fred Smith who co-wrote all the songs with Patti.

The cover photograph was shot by Robert Mapplethorpe and most fans and critics wondered what striking image would grace the comeback sleeve. After the timid withdrawal and coded resignation of *Wave*, it seemed obvious that with Mapplethorpe behind the lens yet again, the comeback image would be strong. Mapplethorpe had taken one potential shot in December 1987 which he felt was perfect. Patti was unsure – she felt he had airbrushed her older looks, and the pair reconvened in early 1988 in Los Angeles where Patti and Fred were temporarily staying in order to complete the lengthy sessions. It was while here that they recorded 'The Jackson Song'. Mapplethorpe was also in Los Angeles and, sensing that Patti was undecided about the earlier photograph, did another shoot. The photographs were developed and raced to Arista, which needed them to meet a deadline. The result is curious. A black and white pose with what appear to be trees or bushes behind Patti. Her hands are awkwardly clasped, as if she isn't comfortable. Her black sweater seems to be stretched, too large for her slender neck. Her hair is braided and her fringe sharp and short. Her face seems strangely untouched by any signs of ageing, the result of some technical 'touching up'. Her eyes look reflective, as if she is troubled by the situation. This may be likely since Mapplethorpe was HIV positive by this stage and becoming increasingly unwell. The image is a polar opposite to the *Horses* cover and strangely inappropriate considering the words "Dream Of Life" – the album's titles – are superimposed next to her photograph. It is as if she was making a veiled comment on the title: what is the dream of life? Her return to the public eye may also explain her uncertain, unsure posture. Was it the right time to return? Would anyone in the fickle pop world still care about her records? Was she compromising the purity of her private life as an artist by re-emerging in an art form she had renounced a la Rimbaud?

The album was widely regarded as a disappointment, both commercially and in content, chiefly because the advance rumours suggested that it would be her strongest record since *Easter*. It was assumed that, with approximately eight years of Patti's creativity saved up, and Fred Smith's reformed MC5 guitar fury, the record would be explosive. It made a minor dent on the sales charts, appearing in the lower reaches of both the US and UK charts during the week beginning July 16, 1988. It fell out of the UK charts after the one week. The first few listens impressed one fact on even the staunchest fan – Lenny Kaye's presence was sorely missed, a fact that mattered a great deal to Fred Patterson: "I was saddened by *Dream Of Life* because Lenny wasn't on it."

There were some amazing songs ('Paths That Cross', 'The Jackson Song', 'Going Under') but the rest of the record seemed bland and unlike anything ever committed to vinyl by Patti before, in parts just plain dull ('Where Duty Calls'). The production was slick and the improvisation that had graced her earlier works seemed to be non-existent; every song seemed meticulously crafted

and recorded. I asked Lee Ranaldo if he had been disappointed by the album, in light of the advance rumours.
He says, "Yes. Don't get me wrong, there are some really
good tracks on that album, but I think the general expec-
tation, however misguided and erroneous it had to be,
was a return to *Horses*-era visionary work, which was
probably impossible. I guess from where I stand I was
sorry that the whole thing wasn't a bit more, uh, challenging maybe, rather than standardised song structures.
But hey, it's still a great album."

The record celebrated the love she had found with
Fred and the family she had made with him – Jackson was
now five and Jesse two. This was most apparent in the
album's haunting closer, the lullaby 'The Jackson Song',
which was written for their son. It was one of two tracks
not recorded at the Hit Factory ('Wild Leaves', the B side
to 'People Have The Power', was recorded in Detroit),
being instead cut in Los Angeles. The piano and vocals
were recorded live and harp and cello overdubbed later.
Patti recalled the extraordinary live take when talking in
1988 to *The Music Paper*: "What happened was that I
missed my cue at the end. I came in a little too late
because I got real moved." The liner notes explain that
the song was recorded on Patti's mother's birthday,
lending the song a larger perspective than just a mother
singing to her son. The song is about the passage of time,
the passing of generations, and the drift from parent to
child to child becoming parent. It is a touching examination of how parenthood only underlines mortality and the
cyclical nature of life, reproduction and, eventually,
death. Some listeners found it shocking to hear something
so cutesy and mumsy from the once 'Punk Poetess', but

the song was a powerful and emotionally charged acceptance of age and nature's ways.

Patti was anxious to remind her audience, via the few
press interviews that she gave, that nine years away had
seen her become a mother and a wife. She made it clear
that *Dream Of Life* was a record that reflected her contemporary concerns and, while she was proud of her four
earlier records, this was a new era. Her lyrical concerns
even embrace the political, with 'Where Duty Calls'
examining the ongoing political problems in Lebanon
though its subject matter seems a little empty and forced.
The lyrics seem to tell a tale about a mother grieving for
her dead son who has surrendered his life for a political
cause, but, curiously, they lack the lightness of touch that
Patti is renowned for. Some fans wondered if Fred had
written this lyric, but that seems unlikely. It ties in with
Genet's obsession with the Palestinian struggle in his last
years, when shortly before his death he stayed in Beirut.
Maybe Patti had decided to adopt Genet's interest in the
political struggles of the Middle East, but she had also
commented that she and Fred spent a lot of time watching
the news on television, and since this was a primary
concern at the time, she may just have been inspired by
the media coverage. The power-poppish 'Looking For
You (I Was)' contains vocal harmonies that hark back to
Patti's love of The Ronettes and also a lyric outlining
what every fan could tell: that Patti had been looking for
her one true love all her life and with Fred she had found
it. The line about the port of Marseille was a reference to
the French town where Rimbaud died and which Genet
frequented.

The first single, 'People Have The Power', an anthemic

slice of power pop, calls on everyone to do their bit to save the world from ruin; an interesting but vague entry into the political arena that Patti had previously avoided. She was also following in Genet's footsteps by turning her creative gaze towards politics: Genet's output after his cessation of novel-writing was centred on papers, articles and speeches in support of his different political interests. Patti told Lisa Robinson in *Interview* in 1988 that she had been reading about Mother Teresa: "Her whole being is to benefit others. That's what inspires me most, seeing people take things in their own hands and not wait for the government to take care of things." She then referred to Elizabeth Taylor's work with AIDS charities, before going on to say: "There are so many responsibilities that we have to assume. And that's what our song 'People Have The Power' is about." Her 'change the world' vibe struck some as a tad hippyish in sentiment, but the song only achieved its full potential when played live on the *Gone Again* tour, when it revealed itself to be both a tribute to Fred's sensitivity and an anthem that musically transcended any corny connotations that the vinyl version had.

The stand-out cut 'Paths That Cross' was written for a friend who had died, Sam Wagstaff, a long-term supporter of Mapplethorpe and his work, as well as one of those who cared most for him. Patti had known Wagstaff through Mapplethorpe for many years and his death in January 1988 prompted the song, which again took on another tone altogether when played live in support of *Gone Again*. In 1988 it was a touching ballad driven by Sohl's keyboards and a graceful lyric that spoke of death as not an end but a place of reunion. By 1995 it was a mournful elegy for everyone who Patti had lost. Patti has often spoken of death as an extension and continuation of the individual's journey, a philosophy that was beautifully addressed in the song. Another death is mentioned in the sleeve notes – that of Andy Warhol, whose passing coincided with the recording of 'Up There, Down There', which, apart from the pure beat-poetry rush of the spoken-word break, was musically and lyrically weak. 'Dream Of Life' is another personal love song to Fred, but again the music dilutes the overall effect. 'Going Under' is another highlight, mixing a heartfelt romantic chain of images to a transcendent piece of music that echoes 'Broken Flag'. The hypnotic power of the spoken word passage proves Patti could still pull out a poetic ace when she wanted, and, as formulaic as her combination of poetry and rock lyric had become, it is still nothing short of astonishing when phrased and structured as beautifully as it is here.

The decision not to tour was due to the couple placing greater importance on raising their children. The 'come-back' came and went, and in 1996 Patti confessed to *Q* magazine a deeper reason for some of the record's lack-lustre material. "When we recorded *Dream Of Life*, it was not entirely artistic," she said. "I was having my second child and it becomes expensive. But my heart wasn't really in a full comeback anyway and the album got no airtime in America." The record failed to re-establish Patti as a legendary artist and in some ways it appeared as though she had lost touch with contemporary music. *Dream Of Life* was an adult rock album, and some of the ideals behind the lyrics seemed rooted in the Sixties and Seventies. It didn't fit either those who remembered her punk-rock tag or the post-punk fans hearing her music for the first time. The record did remind everybody that she still existed, but the decision not to tour, and the luke-warm response from fans and critics, sent Fred and Patti into another era of reclusive writing, studying and parent-hood. They had Jackson and Jesse to raise and Patti was by now insistent that being a wife and a mother were the hardest tasks she had undertaken to date. Also, she was irritated by those who looked down on her for becoming a housewife and mother. Old-school feminist fans viewed her retreat to wifehood and motherhood as a betrayal but, in truth, Patti had control over her life and her destiny, and marriage and motherhood were merely an extension of her personality, something that transcended such narrow feminist arguments. When I asked D.D. Faye if she saw Patti as a feminist, she answered: "Patti Smith is an artist. Relegating a woman to a position of being able to exist only as a feminist or a non-feminist is just as oppressive as relegating her to only the three positions or choices of mother, virgin or whore. She's a human being. What she started was a path. She is still on a path."

Patti wrote constantly while raising her children. She told *The Big 0* in 1995 what she and Fred did between the calm after the release of *Dream Of Life* and the end of the Eighties: "Fred and I had been working. It's a lot more difficult to work when you have a family. We were very devoted parents and that was always our first priority." However, she did go on to explain that her fierce work ethic remained and that her creativity was still aglow. She said: "We were always working at home. It wasn't like we sat at home not doing anything. We still wrote music. I wrote about four books, which in due time I'll be publishing. I was doing a lot of studying and Fred was also. When he wasn't creating music, he became a pilot . . ." Patti and Fred had built a home, a marriage and a family, a series of achievements that Patti saw as more challenging than a rock'n'roll career or a poet's life.

The period after *Dream Of Life* saw the beginning of a series of personal tragedies for Patti that would substantially affect her life and art. Robert Mapplethorpe finally succumbed to a lengthy HIV-related illness and, after developing full-blown AIDS, he died on March 9, 1989. Patti was devastated. The loss of her dear friend and creative anchor would become the subject matter of her book *The Coral Sea* as well as the introduction to the collection of Mapplethorpe photographs that was titled *Flowers*. Not only had Patti lost her oldest friend but the art world had lost a phenomenal talent. Just as she had recognised earlier, the dream of life was merely the flip side of the dream of death.

9

A Season In Heaven And Hell

THE Nineties began ominously with Richard Sohl's death by cardiac seizure on June 3, 1990 in Long Island, New York. He was only 37. Sohl's death followed that of Mapplethorpe the year before, and, with the deaths of Sam Wagstaff and Andy Warhol, was a growing reminder to Patti of the nature of mortality. Patti touched on his death in an interview with *Big O* magazine in 1995: "Richard passed away after we did *Dream Of Life*. He played all the keyboards on *Dream Of Life* with my husband and he passed away in '90 of heart failure. He was wonderful and I was actually quite heartbroken." Fred, who had been talking for some time about a low-key tour featuring Patti, himself, a percussionist and Sohl, was equally devastated.

1990 also saw the release of Patti's first serious piece of published prose – her foreword to the *Flowers/ Mapplethorpe* book which came out in 1990 through Bulfinch Press. Her three-page introduction was a mature and graceful piece of prose that introduced Mapplethorpe's beautiful photographs of flowers. Her style was a far cry from her pre-1979 work and echoed with a soft wistful tone. It was also a place for her to release some of her grief. The prose is touching and, at times, a little like a children's tale or a nursery story, as Patti traces the beauty of the flower over a mini-portrait of Mapplethorpe's life and art. The idea of transience is omnipresent in the tone and Patti concludes by weaving Mapplethorpe's death into the context of all nature, effectively poeticising his memory. The introduction was written in conventional literary form with textbook punctuation and grammar: Patti had accepted form and tradition and was maybe more interested in rejoining the accepted form than trying to challenge it.

Patti's continuing grief over Mapplethorpe was given further release in an acoustic performance of 'People Have The Power' by her and Fred at an AIDS fund-raiser sponsored by Arista records, at Radio City Music Hall in New York. The rest of 1990 and the early part of 1991 were a continuation of the late Eighties lifestyle: reading, studying, writing, raising the children. The ghost of Mapplethorpe's death still lingered in Patti's mind and she dealt with her prolonged sadness by writing a lengthy piece of prose about him that would later be published as *The Coral Sea*. Memories of Mapplethorpe also lay behind another of her rare public appearances at the Nectarine Ballroom in Ann Arbor, Michigan in May 1991, a fundraiser for the Wellness Network's fight against the HIV virus. Patti performed with Lenny Kaye, Jay Dee Daugherty and former Stooges drummer Scott Asheton.

Wim Wenders graced the soundtrack to his 1992 movie *Until The End Of The World* with 'It Takes Time', a rare song by Fred and Patti Smith. The song was primarily Fred's work (he wrote the music and some of the poetry featured in the song's lyrics). It proved to be the only public outing by the couple during 1992. The soundtrack album charted at number 114 on the US album charts during the week of March 9.

The February 1993 issue of *Interview* magazine appeared with an essay by Patti entitled 'February Snow', which remembered Andy Warhol, Robert Mapplethorpe and Richard Sohl. On July 8, 1993, Patti performed in New York's Central Park as part of the Summerstage series. Strictly speaking, it was her first official public appearance since September 1979 (excluding the Detroit Symphony Orchestra benefit in 1980 and the two fundraiser shows). Her contribution, 'Memorial Song', appeared later on the Arista *No Alternative* AIDS benefit album, alongside tracks by contemporary artists such as Pavement, Sonic Youth, Bob Mould, American Music Club, Soul Asylum and Soundgarden. It was a testament to Patti's legacy that she was the only non-contemporary act on the record. It begins as spoken word and talks of her, like many others, losing close loved ones to AIDS. She went on to sing a song that she said she had written shortly before Mapplethorpe died. She sang a cappella in a voice that was obviously close to being overcome with emotion. Patti told *Village Voice* in 1995: "It was one of the happiest nights of my life. I couldn't believe how great these people were. The whole atmosphere not just the audience, but I had my brother there and Fred was there and so I have really happy memories of it."

The third event that made it Patti's busiest year since 1988 was the publication of the pocket-sized collection of nine short pieces of prose, *Wool Gathering*, by Hanuman Books. Patti's title was number 45 in the series, which also included the work of fellow CBCB punk musician-turned-writer Richard Hell. The majority of the stories focus on Patti's childhood, a series of recollections presumably uncovered by watching her own children grow. The language is often simple, bare and sentimental. The black–and–white photographs that grace the inside of the book are by her sister, credited as Linda Smith Bianucci. The content of the mini–stories is personal and reflective; Patti clearly contemplating the meaning of existence throughout these stories, and, via her own children, looking at the world again through a child's eyes. The prose is stark, at times densely poetic and occasionally breaks into verse to highlight a particular couplet or phrase. There are repeated references to her childhood in New Jersey and her brother and sisters frequently populate the tales. Patti seems to typically thinly veil herself as an unnamed character who is obsessed by the fields that lie outside her window. Several of the stories feature a character falling asleep and floating through the windows, where great adventures are had. These experiences are then reported to her fascinated younger brother and sister in the morning. This is of course chiefly based on Patti's real childhood, when she would entertain her brother and sister with flighty tales steeped in a vivid imagination. The image of the wool-gatherers is a sweet childhood recollection: the child probably saw a television show on old-fashioned wool-gathering or saw an image in a book, and is still at an age where they cannot separate information received from real life, hence the curious child looks at night across the fields from his/her bed for the wool gatherers.

The two pieces that aren't part of this cycle on the magic of childhood are different in tone and content.

'Barndance' reads as a third-person meditation, perhaps a collection of late-night thoughts. The other piece offers insight into Patti's life from 1980 to 1991. She describes, in a literal autobiographical manner, a solitary night's activity as she makes tea, listens to old jazz records and draws. The drawing brings back memories of Mapplethorpe and leads into a meditation on creativity. The only fact that questions the timing of the story is the reference to a fire escape which may imply that the piece actually re-creates the time when Patti was living with Mapplethorpe but it may also be her home in Detroit. A fire escape would more typically appear on an apartment block than a family home. Later in the story she drifts into sleep and has a vivid dream. *Wool Gathering* is a document of Patti's life at that time, and is full of meditations on the wonders of being a parent, memories of the parent's own childhood and the general magic of a child's existence which is steeped in innocence, awe and wonder.

The following year, 1994, brought further despair and tragedy for Patti and her family. After the comparatively high-profile activities of 1993, the Smiths returned to their usual private ways. There were two exceptions, however, to the routine. The first was the publication of *Early Work 1970–1979* by W. W. Norton, a compilation of Patti's Seventies poetry which took its selected poems from *Seventh Heaven*, *Kodak*, *Witt* and *Babel*, as well as including rarities such as 'Ha!Ha!Houdini!'. The second exception was that Fred and Patti began talking about a loud guitar-heavy comeback album. The plan was to write some material and record it during the summer of 1995. Some songs were written but the album never came to be. On November 4, the day which would have been Robert Mapplethorpe's birthday, her beloved husband Fred died suddenly of a heart attack. He was only 45 years old.

Her brother Todd immediately arrived in Detroit to stay with her and took her and her two children to New Jersey for the Thanksgiving weekend. Fred and Patti had spent the past 16 Thanksgiving weekends with her parents. Todd spent this one trying to console his sister. He took her out driving during the weekend and played her the soundtrack to *Natural Born Killers* which featured a remix of 'Rock'n'Roll Nigger'. He used the recording to try and convince her that the only way to hold her life together was to start working again. Knowing that he would be her road crew manager, she realised that not only was he right but they could be close while she did it. He talked of quitting his job to do it. To her shock, this turned out to be the last time she saw him – he died of a stroke at the end of December. There is no way of imagining just how horrific and tragic this must have been for Patti.

A tribute concert was held in memory of Fred Smith at The Ark in Ann Arbor, Michigan on April 8, 1995 and Patti appeared briefly at the event. It is possible that this proved to be the catalyst that directed her back to music as a way of being able to carry on in the face of such loss.

Initially, she listened to Bob Dylan's music for comfort and played her acoustic guitar. The recent Dylan album *World Gone Wrong* was the record that she played the most. It was a stripped-down album, featuring Dylan on acoustic guitar, his gnarled voice working through downbeat songs such as 'Blood In Your Eyes'. Strumming soft songs in the basement of her home, she thought of recording a stark acoustic solo record in the tradition of the Dylan albums that she was listening to. The intended rock album no longer seemed appropriate. It also seemed too painful to imagine. Instead, she planned a record that would combine the two musical directions. Lenny Kaye and Jay Dee Daugherty formed the nucleus of the band again and Patti tackled some guitar duties herself. A session musician called Tony Shanahan, best known for his work for John Cale, was drafted in on bass and occasional acoustic guitar. The quartet rehearsed old material and fleshed out a collection of new songs that included 'About A Boy', 'Summer Cannibals' and 'Gone Again'.

Patti returned to live performance with a low-key show at the Phoenix club in Toronto in July 1995. She opened with a reading of her early poem 'Ballad Of A Bad Boy' and went on to premiere 'About A Boy', her Kurt Cobain tribute, as well as a version of 'Dancing Barefoot'. This was a warm-up for her Thursday July 27 concert in New York where she took to the Summerstage, where she had performed in 1993. Much had happened in the meantime and neither Todd nor Fred were there this time. On July 28, she performed an unannounced 45-minute set at the New York site of the travelling Lollapalooza tour, with Jay Dee Daugherty and Lenny Kaye.

Paul Williams recalls hearing about the recording of what would become *Gone Again* from Lenny Kaye in issue 10 of his new, privately subscribed, *Crawdaddy* magazine, and how he dreamed of attending a session at the studio. Unable to make the trip, he remembers instead being at a show by LA band X at the Belly-Up in

Solana Beach when the club announced that they would
be hosting a spoken-word show by Patti Smith. Williams
recounted the event in *Crawdaddy*: "Patti was great. She
was actually as good as I've ever seen, and I saw her and
PSG in 1975–76, in her prime, her glory . . . It was billed
as a spoken-word performance, and it started that way,
and her poetry reading performance was so exquisitely
good I would have been thrilled if there'd been more,
nothing but poetry and prose and talk all evening, and of
course I was also surprised and thrilled that she decided to
share music with us too, a lot of music, with Tony
Shanahan accompanying her on acoustic guitar, and Patti
playing some folk guitar herself, and dancing, oh yes, she
was dancing." Williams goes on to explain the set list:
"She sang 'Dark Eyes' (by Bob Dylan) and 'Dancing
Barefoot' (a great rendition, everyone I've talked to just
loved it) and a new song ('About A Boy' for Kurt Cobain)
and 'Not Fade Away' and something by the Grateful
Dead and 'Ghost Dance' ("we shall live again"), 'The
Jackson Song', 'People Have The Power' and 'Paths That
Cross' – reminding us, the audience, that it's not just Patti
who's back. It's also us."

Patti also read poems for Mapplethorpe and Richard
Sohl as well as giving a rare reading of 'Piss Factory'.
Williams saw the event as having a central theme: "Living
graciously with death and loss. And the vibrant presence
of ancestors and departed friends. So when the club's
phone rang rudely in the distance during her performance
(she'd been mentioning Fred) and she got this attentive
look on her face, I immediately thought, 'She thinks Fred
may be calling her.' She then affirmed that she and I (as
audience) were in tune, by saying, 'He's calling me.'

A moment later, a moth flew by, and she pointed: 'There he goes.'"

Robert Mapplethorpe was still constantly on her mind and when Papermac published Patricia Morrisroe's *Mapplethorpe: A Biography*, she was intrigued to see what Morrisroe had written about her friend. Patti had been interviewed by Morrisroe and contributed scores of memories and recollections. When it came out, she was unhappy with the result, as she recalled to *The Big 0* magazine in 1995: "I think the writer was more interested in a sensationalistic point of view."

Morrisroe revealed what most Patti fans were unaware of, namely that Mapplethorpe and Patti had been young lovers when she first arrived in New York. The affair had been torn apart by Mapplethorpe's homosexuality which was coming to the surface while he was with Patti.

On September 14 Patti participated in the TJ Martell Foundation's 20th anniversary dinner honouring Arista's head, Clive Davis, with the 1995 Humanitarian Award. On October 6, she performed at the Smith Baker Hall in Lowell, Massachusetts in honour of notorious beat writer Jack Kerouac, author of such seminal novels as *On The Road*, *Dr Sax*, *Visions Of Cody*, *The Subterraneans*, *Maggie Cassidy*, *Big Sur* and *The Dharma Bums*. The concerts were in support of the Kerouac Foundation. Sonic Youth's Thurston Moore, Patti and Lenny honoured the writer by visiting his grave before driving to Cambridge where they performed a further two benefit shows at the old Cambridge Baptist Church the following day. All three mini-concerts were performed with Kaye and Moore, who was delighted to be onstage with one of his biggest influences. Moore played guitar on three songs including

a new Patti composition for the occasion and one arrangement which was based around a poem by Kerouac. Patti
paid tribute to Sonic Youth at the Lowell concert when
she read a version of her poem 'high on rebellion', and
dedicated it to the members of the band.

An all-female artist compilation *Ain't Nuthin But A
She Thing* was released on October 24 featuring Patti's
rendition of Nina Simone's 'Don't Smoke In Bed'. On
November 2 she attended a dedication to her husband at a
church in Detroit where there is now a memorial in the
building's bell-tower. She also began to make more and
more frequent trips to New York City, which now held a
curious mix of new and old for her.

The year ended on a spectacular note when Patti's hero
Bob Dylan asked her to open for him on a 10-date US
tour. His gesture was compassionate and thoughtful; as
only another artist could know, he was gently suggesting
that art was her only way to carry on. Just before beginning the tour, and perhaps as a way of calming her nerves,
Patti gave two spoken-word readings at Philadelphia's
Theatre Of The Living Arts on November 24 and 25.

After that she was ready to open for Dylan and The
Paradise Lost Tour with him ran between December 7
and 17, stopping in Connecticut, Massachesetts, New
York and Philadelphia. The tour's title alone was indica-
tive of what had happened to Patti in the past year – she
had lost her paradise with her husband. The Dylan dates
provided a much-needed distraction from the anniversary
of Fred's death and were an offer she couldn't refuse. The
majority of the *Gone Again* album had been recorded at
the Electric Ladyland studios in New York, but hit a
creative block when Patti said she felt she was unable to

continue the sessions. The memory of Fred was too strong. The songs they had been working on, her memories of last being in a studio with Fred, being back in New York with her old bandmates, all opened an array of emotions that enforced a sabbatical on the recording of the record. Patti was able to return to live performance as the opening act for her hero, Bob Dylan. Her band included Tom Verlaine and Lenny Kaye on guitars, Jay Dee Daugherty on drums and Tony Shanahan on bass. Oliver Ray appeared on occasional guitar, while Luis Resto, a Detroit musician, replaced Richard Sohl on keyboards.

Five of these shows were reviewed and covered by Paul Williams in issue number 11 (winter 1996) of *Crawdaddy*. He wrote that he wondered if Patti "might be nervous not only playing a show with Bob Dylan, but also at playing alongside the ghost of her own rock'n'roll legend". After all, it was a challenging way to return to live performance. Not only were the venues relatively high profile, but she was playing with her lifelong hero. She had also listened to Dylan constantly as a means of staying sane during her initial grief over her husband's death. Despite understandable nervousness, Patti and band performed a mixture of electric and acoustic tracks in Danbury, including a version of Dylan's 'Wicked Messenger' which would end up appearing on *Gone Again*. She told the Worcester show audience that she had been nervous and also that: "It's a great honour to play before Bob Dylan." They also treated the crowd to a first ever live performance of 'Up There, Down There' from *Dream Of Life*. Williams recounted Patti's emotional turbulence at returning to the public eye: "The next day she mentioned backstage that it was hard to do these songs, especially the latter, because she felt Fred's presence so strongly when she did, and while that might seem a plus, perhaps the sense of loss was also a distraction (odd to be returning to the stage you had before you were married and suddenly finding yourself missing the special joy of creating music with your late husband)."

For Patti, the shows must have been a mixture of therapy and painful reassessment, and, considering the importance of music in her life with Fred, it must have seemed excruciating to be performing songs that she had originally shaped with him at their home in Detroit. On the other hand, maybe her intention was to reach for the most tangible source of memories with her late husband and by playing specific songs, she was able to remember and feel him most clearly.

Williams recalls that Saturday night's show in Boston (December 9) was when she, as he put it, "stretched her wings". Patti performed previews from the forthcoming *Gone Again* record, as well as 'Not Fade Away' and 'Walkin' Blind' which was her contribution to the movie *Dead Man Walking* which starred Sean Penn and Susan Sarandon. Backstage at the show were Michael Stipe from R.E.M., who had elevated his long term public appreciation of Patti to a sincere and thoughtful friendship, as well as poet Allen Ginsberg. Williams also recounted a fun tale of bassist Tony Shanahan showing lead guitarist Tom Verlaine the chords to 'Rock'n'Roll Nigger', which illustrates that even a guitar legend like Verlaine sometimes needs instruction.

The December 10 show in Boston chalked up another rock milestone – it was the first time Dylan and Patti sang together in public. In a moment which must have been a dream come true for Patti, and an affirmation of her continued status, the pair duetted on Dylan's 'Dark Eyes' and after the song Dylan commented: "A lot of girls have come along since Patti started. But Patti's still the best, you know." Patti and band also premiered 'About A Boy', playing her Cobain tribute for the first time on this tour. The fifth and final show that Williams covered was the December 11 show in New York City, at which Patti rose to the occasion of returning to her roots by opening the show with an unaccompanied reading of 'Piss Factory', thus drawing another perfect circle.

The Paradise Lost tour enabled Patti to contextualise all that had happened to her since she had walked offstage in Florence in September 1979. She was opening for her hero, she was confronting her grief by celebrating the music she had made with her husband, and she was moving forwards in the only way she knew how, by channelling all her pain into powerful art.

The Dylan dates also reintroduced her to the public eye. So many bands and artists had sprung up during her absence and now it was time for Patti's return. Her influence could be seen in countless places, not least in the female punk movement termed Riot Grrrl. Patti was aware of the Riot Grrrls, their punk-inspired self-started network of bands (Bikini Kill, Mudwimin, Huggy Bear, 7 Year Bitch, Tribe 8, Team Dresch, Sleater Kinney), fanzines, conferences, flyers, concerts and records and how their activities revolved around offering young women a cultural community as well as protection from male violence, abusive relationships, sexual abuse, rape, sexism and male suppression. Patti was seen as an icon and figurehead for the Riot Grrrls not only for her music but also because she had challenged a male-dominated record industry by gaining complete artistic control from Arista. Her influence could be felt beyond the Riot Grrrl movement too. British singer/songwriter Polly Harvey struck most listeners when she appeared with her first album in 1990 as a singer/songwriter who had undoubtedly been influenced by Patti. Polly Harvey even looks remarkably similar to the younger Patti, with her long black hair, incredibly skinny body and sharp facial features. The armpit hair debate that had centred around the cover to *Easter* in 1978 was dug up again when Harvey appeared in several photo shoots in British music magazines with visible armpit hair. Harvey's unusual voice was also prone to resemble Patti's extraordinary voice during certain songs but she has long evolved into a highly talented songwriter in her own right.

Courtney Love, musician, singer, songwriter and actress, also drew frequent comparisons to Patti, when she first emerged with her band Hole. Her tonsil-torched voice struck some as reminiscent of vintage live Patti.

Other high-profile fans like Michael Stipe rarely make it through an interview without name-checking Patti, and every time his band R.E.M. used to play in Detroit, he would dedicate a song to her. His debt to her influence is less obvious but still present. He often talks of having scarlet fever as a child and suffering feverish hallucinations, just as Patti did; he rounded off their 'Just A Touch' song with a quote straight off *Easter*, he constructed elaborate stories for journalists and then contradicted them in ensuing interviews and his personal secrecy is reminiscent of Patti's guarded private life. He and Patti eventually became friends after she responded to his long-term public praise for her by sending him a note in early 1995. The pair met and established a strong connection, leading to Stipe travelling with Patti on most of the Dylan dates. Patti sang on the track 'E-Bow The Letter' on R.E.M.'s 1996 album *New Adventures In Hi Fi*.

Michael Stipe is not the only Patti Smith fan in R.E.M. as Peter Buck told me: "I've been a big fan for ever and ever. I used to dress like her during my last year at high school. I went off to college and I was just like the cover of *Horses* – the same haircut – I cut my hair myself. I actually saw her during my last year of school, she played in February of 1976 in Atlanta and it was pretty amazing and really intense. There have been four or five magical moments in my life and that was one of them." He also recounted a touching story from the *Gone Again* tour in 1996: "I got to sit in with Patti. She goes: 'Hey kid, you wanna play this Buddy Holly song with us?' I said, 'Sure, why not!' So I get up in front of 20,000 people and Tom Verlaine's on guitar and she joked: 'Hey kid, can you play?' I said: 'Yeah.' And she said 'Well, you can do all the solos.' And I looked at Tom Verlaine and said 'No Way!' And Patti went, 'What's your name, kid?' And I went, 'Er, Jesse James?' And she said: 'Some punk wants to play with us' and she started playing the song. I stood there knowing that 20 years earlier I'd have given ten years of my life to play rhythm guitar in The Patti Smith Group, being up there trading licks with Lenny Kaye and Tom Verlaine!!"

Other fans include Kristin Hersh, all-girl punk band Babes In Toyland, and Valerie Agnew from 7 Year Bitch. Kim Gordon of Sonic Youth's distinctive, uncompromising vocals are uncannily evocative of premium Patti on such Sonic Youth tracks as 'Brave Men Run', 'Protect Me You', 'Flower', 'Shadow Of A Doubt', 'Starpower' and 'Halloween'. Carla Bozulich is another artist who regularly name-checks Patti as a huge influence. And Sonic Youth's Thurston Moore and Lee Ranaldo are also both huge fans.

1996 was to be the year that Patti Smith reclaimed her crown as the Queen of the rock poets and *Gone Again* was scheduled to be her strongest record since *Easter*. She had remained strong and written the record that Fred had wanted: a loud rock album that would re-introduce her to a new audience unfamiliar with her work and also recontextualise her with the younger artists who were generating work inspired by her legacy.

10

Back Again

PATTI Smith's most high-profile year since 1979 began with the release of the *Dead Man Walking* movie soundtrack on January 9. Her contribution was 'Walkin' Blind'. The film concerned a character played by Sean Penn who is waiting to be executed. Patti's response to all the death that had happened around her was to adopt a new philosophy that while we're alive on this planet we must do all we can do. Her painful lessons about mortality had taught her to appreciate the present tense and with this in mind, 1996 was destined to be a busy and productive year.

The release of the soundtrack was closely followed by her return to the glitz of the music industry on January 17 when she attended the 11th ceremony of the Rock And Roll Hall Of Fame. The Induction dinner was held at the Waldorf Astoria Hotel in New York and Patti was there to induct The Velvet Underground. At the after dinner jam, Patti performed 'Pale Blue Eyes', a song she had covered for many years, which comes from the third Velvet Underground album. The third important moment in a hectic month was winning the 'Most Welcome Comeback' award in the annual *Rolling Stone* magazine

Critics' Poll. This award was a critical testimony to the importance of her work, past, present and future. Her so-called comeback seemed vital compared with lame 'comeback' tours peddled by the likes of The Sex Pistols. David Fricke offered some insight into the *Rolling Stone* award and why her return outshone the profit-driven tour by The Sex Pistols: "I can't speak for all the other writers who voted in that category but my personal feeling is that, of all the Seventies punk-era artists who returned to action, she was one of the few, if not the only one, who had something original to say to a new audience as well as those who had stuck with her through all that time. The Sex Pistols, for instance, as musicians and as people, frankly, they never went away – they're careerists. Patti Smith has come and gone and come back again when she felt she had something to say. If you want to compare what The Sex Pistols achieved in 1996 with what Patti Smith achieved in 1996, you have a live record of old hits versus a new record about the passage through grief and finding some sort of new optimism in very troubled times. And The Sex Pistols, they came back for the money, Patti Smith didn't come back for the money. She came back because she had something she had to get out and something difficult to get out: loss and a lot of hard work."

The shows that paved the way for her true 'comeback' album couldn't have been further away from The Sex Pistols' tour. The reviews were glowing, the performances were raw and passionate and, unlike the Pistols, the tickets actually sold out. The shows were fitted around the school schedules of her two children: Patti and band played in San Francisco on March 18 and 19, Los Angeles on March 20 and 23 and San Diego on March 27. Just over a week later Patti took part in the Jewel Heart Benefit concert, appearing alongside beat poet Allen Ginsberg. When this initial warm-up tour ended, the children's schooling dictated a two-month break, which would end when Patti made her first appearance in the UK since September 1979.

Patti's return to the public eye in the UK occurred as part of a three-day conference entitled Incarcerated With Artaud And Genet at London's ICA (Institute Of Contemporary Arts) which ran from May 31 to June 2. The conference was a celebration of the work and legacy of two artists that Patti had long respected. Patti's first ever live poetry reading in New York had been dedicated to Jean Genet, and as she had discovered her artistic voice via the work of other artists, it was fitting that her return to public performance in London and Europe should be part of an event celebrating Genet and Artaud. The event ran over a weekend during which varying speakers and performers celebrated the tenth anniversary of Genet's death and the centenary of Artaud's birth. Patti was attracted to the ICA's reputation for excellent arts events and she appeared alongside the likes of Moroccan writer Tahar Ben Jelloun, who was a friend of Genet's for the last part of his life, and film-maker Alejandro Jodorowski.

On the Friday afternoon of the conference, Patti gave an hour-long talk about how she viewed Artaud and Genet and how Genet in particular had influenced her own work. The moment completed a full circle from her first New York poetry reading in 1971 which was dedicated to him, to a point in her life 25 years later when his work was still vital to her being. On the Saturday morning, she attended the conference as an audience member, especially to see Tahar Ben Jelloun. The acoustic performance on Saturday night was an exclusive one-off gig for the lucky hundred or so who had tickets. The ICA had charged £40 for a day ticket (£35 for ICA members) and £100 for a weekend pass (£90 for members). Patti's gig was for holders of the weekend ticket only, thus making her performance an elitist event for those who could afford the ticket price. She argued that her so-called 'gig' was only for Artaud and Genet, and therefore not a music event but instead a way for her to pay homage to her influences. Patti performed a mixture of poetry and songs (new and old) with Oliver Ray and Lenny Kaye.

The day after, June 3, Arista UK held a private invitation-only party for 200 guests at the Serpentine Gallery in London, to celebrate Patti's return and to premiere the new album to a select audience crammed full of the media elite. The third part of her London visit was a television appearance. Patti and Lenny Kaye appeared on Jools Holland's live music show on June 8, when Patti read 'People Have The Power' and then she and Lenny played a raw and incandescent acoustic version of 'Gone Again'. It was a menacingly stark blues song, a teasing taste of the forthcoming album. Patti looked dishevelled and visibly older. She sat at the piano and spoke briefly with Holland, appearing quiet, respectful and humble. (The same pair of songs were performed later in the summer on the US TV show *Saturday Night Special*, and Patti also appeared on the US David Letterman show playing 'Summer Cannibals'.)

Released into the stores at the same time as the new album was Patti's book for Mapplethorpe, *The Coral Sea*, just one of the unpublished books that Patti had written since *Dream Of Life*. The weight of the subject, Robert Mapplethorpe, and the power of Patti's reputation led to publisher W.W. Norton securing two famed artists to provide quotes on the book's back cover. One was Patti's long term hero William S. Burroughs and the other was Edmund White, who had also written an acclaimed biography of Jean Genet.

W.W. Norton had also published her *Early Work* in 1994. Patti's tight, poetic and often dense prose resonates with a grace of word that makes it clear to readers new to her work that her background was in writing poetry. The work is split into 20 brief sections and running throughout, between and alongside her prose, are a series of black-and-white photographs by Mapplethorpe. The prose remembers and mourns him. Whereas the introduction to the 1990 *Flowers* book had been a celebration of the life and art of Mapplethorpe, this is a deep meditation on the journey he made to his death. Patti regularly travelled from Detroit to New York to see him when he was sick, and as he approached his death she visited him for one last time. When it was time for her to leave, he had fallen asleep, therefore leaving her with an everlasting memory of him sleeping. *The Coral Sea* charts his movement towards death in mournful and poetic prose, each word heavy with grief and memories.

Gone Again was released into record stores in the US on June 18, 1996. The cover portrait is the most intensely private of the six sleeve photographs to date. Patti's face is almost hidden by her hand and her hair. The contrast between this and the sleeve to *Dream Of Life* is extreme. The soft-faced Patti that stared out in 1988 was replaced

by a person washed over with grief. Patti is contempla-
tive, hidden. This photograph was taken by Annie
Leibovitz, known among Patti fans for her legendary
Rolling Stone cover shot in 1978 which posed Patti in
front of roaring flames.

Musically, *Gone Again* is a raw blues album, drawing on
a rough but steady production sound, courtesy of
Malcolm Burn and Lenny Kaye. It is a blues album in the
most traditional sense – not in its musical legacy but in
the expression of loss, despair and pain through music.
The guitar sounds pick up where *Wave* left off, making it
clear that the main problem with *Dream Of Life* was that
Kaye wasn't playing guitar on any of the tracks. *Gone
Again* listed not only Lenny's blazing contribution but
also some delicate fretwork by Patti's long time friend,
Tom Verlaine. The bass guitar slot was filled by Tony
Shanahan, most commonly known for his work as John
Cale's bassist. Jay Dee Daugherty was still drumming, but
keyboards were played by Luis Resto, who replaced
Richard Sohl. Haunting cello was added to 'My Madrigal'
by Jane Scarpantoni, a session musician most famed for
her work with R.E.M., Nirvana and Minneapolis singer/
songwriter Bob Mould. Oliver Ray, who shot the
booklet photography, also played guitar and whistle on
several of the songs.

The album's opening track, 'Gone Again', is one of
two songs written by Fred and Patti, the other being the
single 'Summer Cannibals'. 'Summer Cannibals' evokes
comparisons with Dylan's 'All Along The Watchtower',
while 'Gone Again' stomps with a drumbeat and guitar
riff that Led Zeppelin would have been proud of – it also
gives the clearest idea of the raw rock album Fred and

Patti were planning. 'Summer Cannibals' proved an unlikely song to release as a single, with its surreal chorus, but it appeared with a promo video shot by Robert Frank. The songwriting period that followed Fred's death had seen Patti drifting towards a Dylan-esque acoustic folk-blues sound. Evidence of this can be heard on the acoustic tracks credited to Patti alone: 'Dead To The World', 'Farewell Reel' and 'Ravens'. Her plan soon altered, thus making way for two of her compositions with Fred, a selection of acoustic folk songs, and a mix of powerful band efforts that resulted from her collaborations with Lenny Kaye.

Curiously, the album was recorded in New York City's Electric Ladyland studios, where her musical career had begun with the recording of 'Piss Factory/Hey Joe'. The curiosity stems from the fact that Patti has never been interested in looking back, so it was unusual for her to return to the very beginning of her musical story, and even employ some of the same team, Lenny Kaye and Tom Verlaine. It was, presumably, a symbolic move on Patti's part, the message being that she had been forced to start over again. Lyrically, she was struggling with loss and grief. Her art provided a channel for the welter of emotions bubbling inside her. Fred had been teaching Patti to play guitar before he died, and this musical legacy adds to the poignancy of 'Farewell Reel', the record's closing track and the most specific tribute to the memory of her husband. Over an acoustic guitar strum that could have graced any one of Bob Dylan's albums, Patti mournfully addresses Fred.

'Beneath The Southern Cross' is also underpinned by an acoustic guitar, but embellished by John Cale's organ playing, Tom Verlaine's ghostly guitar and Jeff Buckley's choirboy harmonising. Patti's lyric links directly with the narrative of *The Coral Sea*, which tells the tale of a dying man travelling to fulfil his final wish – to see the Southern Cross. The issue of mortality rides high in the subject matter. Patti is undoubtedly questioning what it means to be here, living, and how fragile the connection is between life and death. This is followed by the dirge-droning of 'About A Boy', which pays tribute to Kurt Cobain, Nirvana's ill-fated front man. The surging guitars build in intensity, and end up sounding like a cross between Neil Young and Sonic Youth at their most conventional, courtesy of Oliver Ray's guitar feedback. The eerie atmospherics are reminiscent of the *Rising* album by Yoko Ono, who, like Cobain's widow Courtney Love and Patti, eventually took her grief to a select live audience in 1996. Another similarity between the two artists was evident when both appeared live with their sons. Patti showcased Jackson's guitar-playing live with a cover of Deep Purple's 'Smoke On The Water' while Yoko's live band, IMU, were lead by Sean Lennon. I asked David Fricke, who had covered the re-emergence of Yoko Ono both on record and live, whether he saw similarities between the two women. Fricke answered, "You could draw similarities between the two, but I think actually they're fundamentally very different people in their styles, their expression, and what it is they're getting out, but the one thing that really is very similar is that they were both utterly devoted to their husbands."

Patti's devotion to her husband is the topic of 'My Madrigal'. It would appear to have come from the same musical lineage as 'Paths That Cross' and 'We Three', with Patti singing a sombre verse over a delicate piano and Scarpantoni's cello. The main lyrical hook revolves around a marriage vow and the scattered verse mournfully recalls a time when her lover was alive and ponders the significance of personal commitment in later life. It is without doubt the most affecting track on the album, particularly with its repeated closing couplet. If 'We Three' had been deconstructed doo-wop, then this was funereal doo-wop. It's raw and acutely personal, a pained meditation on marriage vows.

The lyric of 'Wings' is constructed around a line borrowed from her earlier poem 'Wing', which appeared in the *Early Work* collection in 1994. A lazy acoustic waltz backs another examination of grief, this time focusing bitterly on the loss. Imagining a time when there was nobody and nothing to lose, she sings sadly of that absence of potential loss.

Its acoustic predecessor 'Dead To The World' had a lighter, more jaunty beat, but some felt Patti's vocal owed just a little too much to Bob Dylan's famous nasal twang. The whistles in the middle eight sound like a break from a spaghetti western, but the portrait of crippling grief clashes with the upbeat music. Patti's sister Kimberly (who is also a musician) plays mandolin to Patti's acoustic guitar. Patti's pledge to the moment is a direct result of the sudden deaths of those close to her and the constant threat of death is what gives her life meaning and urgency.

The cover of Dylan's 'Wicked Messenger' is an opportunity to pay homage to the effect his music has had on her entire adult life. His records helped her through her initial grief after the deaths of her husband and brother and his offer to tour with him inspired and motivated her.

Patti's tribute to his presence in her life is evident in the number of lyric lines she spits out on this album in a Dylan-esque whine. 'Wicked Messenger' is a song that Patti had been performing since the Paradise Lost shows and its presence is related to both its personal significance to her and the inspiration she had recently drawn from Dylan and his music.

'Fireflies' and 'Farewell Reel' are the heart and soul of the album. 'Fireflies' clocks in at nine minutes and 33 seconds, making it even longer than 'About A Boy'. It is the most intense song on the record. Unusual percussion and haunting guitar create a ghostly mood, over which Patti opens the song with humming and moaning, akin to the trancelike patterns of prayer or deep meditation. She sounds numb and in deep shock. The delivery and phrasing draw from the purest blues music, while the lyrics make the listener feel as if they have access to the thoughts of someone deep in prayer. Throughout and around the lyrics reprinted on the album's liner notes, Patti counts down on a buried vocal track. Imagining that 'Fireflies' took her to the farthest point of being alive, 'Farewell Reel' is the message that she leaves at this midway point between life and death, rendering her able to return to life.

Gone Again is an extraordinary attempt to rationalise death and grief. Patti asks the question: how does a person carry on when their loved ones die? It is an exploration of the human survival instinct – in this case, her survival is linked to her art and her family. Patti dealt with her loss through her art. She wrote *The Coral Sea* to exorcise her grief over Robert Mapplethorpe's death. She wrote *Gone Again* as a means of remembering her husband and as a

Patti Smith in concert in Detroit, 1978. ROBERT MATHEU/RETNA LTD/CORBIS

Patti Smith performing in the parking lot of the Sunset Boulevard Licorice Pizza record store, Los Angeles, on May 11, 1978.
MICHAEL OCHS ARCHIVE/GETTY IMAGES

Patti Smith hanging out with Lou Reed, 1978. LYNN GOLDSMITH/CORBIS

Patti Smith with her parents, Beverly (left) and Grant (right) in Philadelphia, 1981. ROBERT MATHEU/RETNA LTD/CORBIS

Patti Smith with her mother Beverly (centre) and sister Kimberly (right) LYNN GOLDSMITH/CORBIS

Patti Smith performing with her husband Fred 'Sonic' Smith at Arista Records' 15th Anniversary Concert AIDS fundraiser, Radio City Music Hall, March 17, 1990. ROBIN PLATZER/TWIN IMAGES/TIME LIFE PICTURES/GETTY IMAGES

Patti Smith performing with her husband Fred 'Sonic' Smith at Arista Records' 15th Anniversary Concert AIDS fundraiser, Radio City Music Hall, March 17, 1990. EBET ROBERTS/GETTY IMAGES

Patti Smith performing 'Dark Eyes' with Bob Dylan at the Beacon Theater in New York City, December 14, 1995. EBET ROBERTS/GETTY IMAGES

Patti Smith with writer William S. Burroughs, September 1995, snapped by poet Allen Ginsberg. ALLEN GINSBERG/CORBIS

Patti Smith plays guitar next to her son Jackson (R), on March 27, 2008 at the exhibition Patti Smith, Land 250 at the Fondation Cartier in Paris. FRANCK FIFE/AFP/GETTY IMAGES

Patti Smith pictured at the concert staged for the final night of CBGBs club, New York City, October 15, 2006. L-R: Tony Shanahan, Jay Dee Daugherty, Patti Smith and Lenny Kaye. RAHAV SEGEV/RETNA LTD/CORBIS

Patti Smith with Edward Mapplethorpe at the private view of the Robert Mapplethorpe exhibition Still Moving And Lady, at the Alison Jacques Gallery, London, September 7, 2006. REX FEATURES

Patti Smith and Michael Stipe of R.E.M. duet on 'I Wanna Be Your Dog'/ 'People Have The Power' at the 22nd Annual Ro & Roll Hall of Fame Induction Ceremony, New York City, March 12, 2007. JEFF KRAVITZ/FILM MAGIC

Keith Richards and Patti Smith performing together at the 22nd Annual Rock & Roll Hall of Fame Induction Ceremony, in New York City, March 12, 2007. DAVID ATLAS /RETNA LTD/CORBIS

Patti Smith and her children, Jesse (left) and Jackson (right), with Steven Sebring (far right), director of *Patti Smith: Dream Of Life* at the documentary's premiere at the Sundance Film Festival in Park City, Utah, January 14, 2008. FERNANDO LEON/RETNA LTD/CORBIS

Patti Smith, in New York City, 2010. MATTIA ZOPPELLARO

way of coping with her loss. It is also the completion of a project that she was planning with Fred, thus making the record a tribute to him.

The record was met with mostly positive reviews, but some critics who couldn't tolerate someone with Patti's reputation returning at the age of 49 felt obliged to tear her down. One example was the review of *Gone Again* that appeared in *Spin* magazine which summed up the record as being: "as raw and self-indulgent as most art-as-therapy". It would appear they missed the point of the album and saw it as one woman's grief rather than a universal examination of death. *Time Out New York*'s Gail O'Hara called it "a tender, personal testament to her marriage", which, while still missing the heart of the record, was at least getting closer. Lee Ranaldo saw the content as logical: "I like the record a lot, maybe because it has the feeling of personal statement. What else could she have done after such a tragic year, but turn back to what she knows best and relieve her grief and celebrate her loved ones through music?"

Now that Patti's public comeback was in full swing, a trio of US shows were booked around the kids' schooling. A close-to-home concert was performed at Pine Knob, Michigan, followed by a pair of warm-up shows for the impending European tour at New York's Irving Plaza venue, on June 21 and 22. The European tour began where Patti's commitment to art had been finalised in summer 1972: Paris. Patti and band played on July 2 and 3 before breaking for three weeks. Gossip columnists were quick to notice that the audience contained a major fan: fashion designer Ann Demeulemeester.

Patti's juggling of motherhood and this rock tour was a

means of preventing her from becoming caught up in the rock'n'roll circus as she had been before. Once school had broken for the summer they were able to play in Ostend, Belgium on July 24. Her triumphant return to the UK was next on the agenda and the mini-tour began on August 5 at the Royal Concert Hall in Glasgow. Working their way down the country, they played the next night at the Labatt's Apollo in Manchester and then down to London for two shows at the Shepherd's Bush Empire on August 7 and 8. The show on August 7 caught Patti on a turbulent high. Her neck, which still bothers her regularly, nearly 20 years after the Tampa fall, was causing her pain and the dates were nearly cancelled because she didn't think she'd be able to make it through. Thankfully she was OK and opened the show with a reading of 'Piss Factory' that made it instantly clear that age had only added to her intensity. Tom Verlaine sat casually to one side of the stage and brushed fragments of magnificent guitar whenever the moment took him. Lenny Kaye was so enthusiastic that it was a pleasure to watch – somebody who clearly loves his job more than anything. He even sang lead vocal on a (hopefully) tongue-in-cheek rip through Deep Purple's 'Smoke On The Water'. Patti's son, Jackson, played lead guitar on this rendition and looked every bit the teenage Jimi Hendrix. Patti crouched on the edge of the stage and stared wistfully at her son, her eyes betraying some deep sentiments. It was a powerful moment for her as a mother but also because she must have seen her late husband in their creation.

The memory of those Patti had lost was a constant presence, especially in the versions of 'Ghost Dance' and 'Paths That Cross'. Her between-song monologues were varied in mood and tone. She recalled meeting Bob Dylan, and how he wanted to know what this poem 'dog dream' that he'd heard she'd written about him was about. She laughed as she remembered telling him that she didn't know. The mood changed and she seemed close to breaking down when she remembered her brother Todd, who had always been the band's road manager and therefore was sorely missed now they were touring. She recalled how much he had loved London. At moments like this, she fell silent and everybody in the theatre knew what she was thinking. She lightened the mood by re-telling the famous story of how a Sex Pistol had attacked Todd in New York with a bottle. It was during Sid Vicious' final days and he'd started an argument with Todd and smashed a bottle in his face. Todd had needed stitches but had gone down in punk-rock history, because Vicious died shortly afterwards. Musically, the band was razor sharp and when they played 'Redondo Beach' half the place was jumping for joy.

The second of the London dates featured a special guest appearance by John Cale. The final date on the short but successful European tour was in the Swedish capital of Stockholm on August 9.

Returning to the States, the band played a mini-festival in Boulder, Colorado, before the school terms began again and dates were restricted as before. Patti accepted an invitation to be a guest speaker at the College Music Journal Conference in New York (put on by the magazine of the same name, known as *CMJ*) on September 5. The next day she and the band played a blistering set at the Central Park Summerstage in New York, thus maintaining what was fast becoming an annual appointment at the venue. Next up was a three-date opening slot for another legend, this time Neil Young, in Los Angeles on September 11, Irvine on September 12 and The Gorge in Oregon on September 14. Another break occurred due to the demands of motherhood, and then in October they played three charity shows. The first was the Lifebeat concert on October 12 in Washington DC. The other two were both in San Francisco for Young's cerebral palsy charity. The annual concerts (which go under the title of the Bridge Benefit Concerts) are organised by Young, whose own children suffer from the illness. Patti's involvement was a natural extension of the dates she'd played with Neil Young and Crazy Horse.

The rest of the year featured only two low-key dates, one at Nightingales in New York on Halloween and the other in the first week of November at New York's Museum Of Modern Art. The MOMA show ran in association with the Museum's exhibition of drawings by Antonin Artaud, an artist who Patti had already celebrated at the ICA in London at the beginning of summer. Patti had put forward the suggestion that she perform in Artaud's honour, but also to raise the profile of the exhibition. Having been exposed to three days of rabid Artaud discourse at the ICA, she felt more than confident about singing his praises. She performed in a black hooded coat, thus giving her the image of a mystic or a visionary. Then she proceeded to read a selection of Artaud's writings and some of her own. To punctuate the spoken words, she also performed a selection of songs, backed up by acoustic guitar from Oliver Ray.

The event also had a private sense of homecoming for Patti. She had made the difficult decision of moving back to New York City. The MOMA show came just as she had returned to Manhattan's energetic sprawl. She and her two children, who were now 14 (Jackson) and nine (Jesse), moved into temporary accommodation at the Chelsea Hotel while they waited for the mortgage for their new home to be finalised. Few of her old New York acquaintances could believe that an active artist like Patti was best suited to a lakeside suburb in Detroit, but it was always clear that she was there because of love, not because of personal preference. The move back to New York, the city she always referred to as her adopted home, seemed obvious on some levels: she could be near Lenny Kaye and other close friends; she needed to be able to rehearse with the band if her rock career was to continue; and, to re-emerge as a still relevant artist, she needed the inspiration of the city. It was also an opportunity to leave painful memories behind and to start afresh. On a more peculiar level, it appeared that she was dealing with her ongoing grief by returning to the safety of the pre-Fred days. *Gone Again* had been recorded at Electric Ladyland studios, thus providing a full circle in her musical career and now, in November 1996, she had moved into the Chelsea Hotel with her two children. Patti had found herself as an artist at the Chelsea Hotel; it was where she plotted her career with Mapplethorpe. So much had happened to her there that it seemed as if she were returning to her memories.

The choice of the Chelsea may have seemed strange but was typical of Patti's strong character: it seemed more as if she had deliberately chosen the hotel as a means of confronting old ghosts and faces. This seems highly likely as she was also on the eve of her 50th birthday, an occasion that guarantees plenty of reflection in everyone's life. Again, the myth that surrounds Patti (and is the direct result of her 'retirement' having frozen her legend in fans' memories) makes it hard to realise that she could have turned 50; it is difficult to think of many female singers who would still be regarded as vital artists, 25 years after they first appeared in the public eye. Patti, however, had always defied the traditional 'sexy, good-looking' stereotype that most record labels use to sell their female artists, and consequently saved herself from the indignity of watching her career wane in proportion to her looks. She ended the chaos of 1996 by moving into her new home, and spent a quiet Christmas period with her family back in New York City.

11

On The Road

NOW that Patti was again part of the city that never sleeps, she started the year as she no doubt meant to go on. A tour of Japan and Australia had been planned for some time and was finally pencilled in for January. The band played two warm-up dates at the 9:30 club in Washington DC before flying to Japan. The Japanese shows began with a pair of dates on January 8 and 9 at the Nakano Sun Plaza in Tokyo. The band remained in Tokyo but switched to the Ebisu Garden Hall for another pair of dates on January 11 and 12. They travelled to Osaka for the January 14 concert at Kouseinenkin Kaikan. Finally they returned to the Ebisu Garden Hall for a sixth date on January 16. The set list was noted by Mutsuko Nagai and was as follows: 'People Have The Power' (spoken word), 'Gone Again', 'Wicked Messenger', 'Redondo Beach', 'Kimberly', 'Radio Ethiopia', 'Dancing Barefoot', 'Ghost Dance', 'Beneath The Southern Cross', 'Walkin' Blind', 'Common People', 'Summer Cannibals', 'About A Boy', 'Because The Night', 'Wing', 'People Have The Power', 'Not Fade Away' and, as an encore, 'Rock'n'Roll Nigger'.

Mutsuko Nagai, a Japanese fan and then manager of a

record store in Osaka, explained to me the significance of the Osaka concert for Japanese fans. "Patti Smith didn't come to Japan in the Seventies. We, the Japanese, had to wait for about 20 years to see her legendary live performance. Following the release of *Gone Again*, when it was announced that Patti Smith was coming to Japan to play, most of her fans felt happy and anxious at the same time, because we wondered whether she had been rocking or whether she had changed completely. Patti didn't ever have any big hits in Japan and she was regarded as a has-been. What we occasionally heard about her was only sad news – that people around her were dying, one after another. Although she was going to play at bigger venues than bands like Nirvana and Smashing Pumpkins, the tickets still sold out completely. To be honest, I was a bit surprised about it and ended up waiting for the day with a little tension."

Many fans were in the same position as Nagai and were apprehensive about seeing their idol for the first time. Mostly it was a direct result of the myth that surrounds her name. For fans who had never been able to see her or who had discovered her records after 1980, the anticipation was not dissimilar to the Velvet Underground reunion tour, where many fans debated whether or not to possibly sacrifice their unblemished view of the band by seeing a much older version of the original. Japanese fans were worried that, after all the tragic events that had happened to Patti, and with her now being 50 years old, perhaps she might be less powerful or intense than in the era that her myth sprang from. Nagai, speaking for the Japanese fans who saw these concerts, was not disappointed by Patti. "Finally when she appeared on the stage, she was received with heart-wrenching shouts of joy and bursts of applause. As soon as she began to sing, the audience showed their appreciation for her. The woman who was standing on the stage with bare feet was more powerful than we had imagined. Her voice touched us. I saw a lot of fans shed tears, including me. It is difficult for us to understand her words because we aren't familiar with the Bible. However, we did appreciate her spirit. Everyone who was in the venue strongly believed in it. Her spirit was deeply etched in our minds and we felt convinced that we would never lose it. Patti played Japanese traditional instruments and performed with an arrow which is used at traditional ceremonies. 'About A Boy' was sung not for Kurt Cobain but as a story of a young Japanese monk. The moment she said, 'I've never played electric guitar since 1979, thank you for inspiring me' and strummed on her electric guitar was the climax of this show."

Nagai went on to touch upon the undeniably spiritual and inspiring feel of a live Patti Smith concert: "Everyone was proud of themselves after the show because we saw Patti's performance and not The Sex Pistols' reunion. We appreciated her for letting us know that getting old wasn't sad, but beautiful. We are back to normal life again. However, we have taken her spirit and soul in our minds. I'm sure everyone will keep her spirit with them when they are in their graves. What she showed us was the incarnation of soul, which led us to be like ourselves. My message to Patti from Japanese fans is: We are most grateful to you. You let us get over the wall of language between the Americans and the Japanese and then you reminded us of something we have forgotten."

The band then travelled to Australia for three shows, including a pair in Sydney on January 21 and 22. After the third date on January 24, they flew back to the US, where they appeared during the first week of February on the high-ratings David Letterman show. Patti then continued the band's commitment to supporting causes they found valuable by performing at the Tibet House New York Benefit Concert at a sold-out Carnegie Hall on February 17. It was the fifth of the annual Free Tibet concerts. Patti appeared alongside Natalie Merchant (who had recently covered 'Because The Night' with her former band 10,000 Maniacs and scored a hit single), R.E.M.'s Michael Stipe, John Cale, beat poet Allen Ginsberg and the Drepung Loseling Monks, who opened and closed the evening with their haunting chanting. Merchant performed a new composition with composer Philip Glass. Patti sang backing vocals on Michael Stipe's rendition of R.E.M.'s recent collaboration with Patti, 'E-Bow The Letter'. Other musicians included Billy Corgan, singer/guitarist from The Smashing Pumpkins, and LA-based new blues-folk singer Ben Harper. Patti's main contribution was a rousing, optimistic performance of 'People Have The Power'.

Now that Patti was making it clear that 1997 would be no quieter or less chaotic than 1996, she realised that she needed to launch a new image that encapsulated her position as an icon. This re-dressing of Patti Smith came via the most unexpected of places – the fashion catwalks. Patti appeared in several high-profile fashion magazines during the month of February 1997. She appeared in the March UK editions of *Harper's Bazaar* and *Elle*. Both magazines were paying attention to the spring and summer 1997 fashion lines that had been premiered in Paris. A hot ascending designer based in Antwerp called Ann Demeulemeester made it clear that her new lines were influenced by punk and especially by Patti Smith. Demeulemeester confessed that she was an enormous fan and had organised her personal schedules throughout 1996 around Patti Smith concerts. This long-term affection for Patti led her to put models onto a premiere catwalk in outfits that resembled the cover of *Horses*: models with plain white masculine-looking shirts and ties casually thrown around their necks and hanging loose. It was a masculine–feminine image that Patti had trademarked in 1975. Thirty years later, at the age of 50, she was no longer a gawky youth (she would have beem 20) turning to the Paris catwalks for dreams and inspiration, but instead the inspiration behind a designer's 1997 lines. Both *Elle* and *Harper's Bazaar* ran the *Horses* cover image alongside their reports. *Elle* ran Patti's picture next to pictures of Marlene Dietrich and Diane Keaton, who were also both wearing ties.

Patti's re-emergence as a style icon wasn't restricted to Europe: she also appeared in the American fashion magazine *W* and in the Japanese style and culture magazine *Cut* (subtitled *International Interview Magazine*). *W* magazine ran a 12-page fashion spread and interview in its January 1997 issue. The interview was conducted with Patti while she was temporarily holed up in the Chelsea Hotel and primarily addressed issues that centred on her 50th birthday: ageing, the loss of friends, grief over her husband's death and the importance of her children. The photospread was fascinating, with Patti's revolutionary tomboy look now an acceptable fashion statement. The opening

double-page black-and-white photograph featured a con-
templative, eyes closed, whirling Patti; her arms outstretched as she danced on the beach at Coney Island in a
baggy Demeulemeester sweater. The other Coney Island
shots were more in keeping with the recent catwalk
re-creation of the *Horses* cover.

The main coloured double-page spread seems to be
loosely based on the cover to the Bob Dylan album
Bringing It All Back Home. Patti was photographed in her
room at the Chelsea Hotel wearing a red dress and the
kind of checked shirt popularised by grunge. Her head is
tilted back and her face buried under a mass of messed-up
hair. She is playing an acoustic guitar. In the background
of the blurred, soft-focus shot is a microphone stand, a
black hat and a worn copy of one of Jean Genet's five
novels, *Querelle*, which indicates that Genet is still a huge
part of her life. Another series of black-and-white photographs show her in a knee-length dress and heavy army
boots with no laces. Her lightning-flash tattoo is still
visible on her left knee. The photographs are a curious
document of her current image that retain an inevitable
reference to her earlier looks. Perhaps this was a sub-
conscious result of the spread photographer being Steven
Sebring, who would in 2008 release his documentary,
Patti Smith Dream of Life.

Even when she is dressed up in designer clothes and
posing for a fashion magazine, Patti Smith still defiantly
clings to her values and ideals, as became clear in the
fashion shoot that appeared in issue 3, number 58 of
Japan's *Cut* magazine. The feature was 12 pages long, and
was a re-run of the US *Interview* feature that had appeared
in June 1996. Two pages were made up of black-and-

white photographs of Patti and Robert Mapplethorpe, while the current colour pictures were all based around the *Horses* cover image – white shirt, dark blue tie, black jacket. Two pictures showed a sneering, almost disgusted-looking Patti, who posed with grey streaked unkempt hair, a white crumpled T-shirt with 'Tokyo' emblazoned on the front and highly visible upper-lip hair. It was a self-referential gesture towards the *Easter* armpit hair cover shot and, again, Patti's message was loud and clear: why should I remove my upper-lip hair just to suit a social code? Consequently the image was ambiguous, with her male dress and masculine looks underlined by a visible moustache. Even at the age of 50, Patti was clearly determined to continue the gender debates that had raged inside her head all of her life.

Lenny Kaye made a brief appearance with Jim Carroll at the Statler-Auditorium of Cornell University, where he played guitar in support of the musical half of Carroll's spoken-word set. It was an increasingly rare side project for Kaye, who was spending more and more time working on the new Patti record. An Allen Ginsberg album also surfaced around this time, which Kaye had produced in 1996, working around the tight *Gone Again* schedule. The following week, Patti and Oliver Ray made a surprise appearance at a tiny club called Rivoli (capacity 150) in Toronto, on Saturday March 8. Ray played acoustic guitar and the performance only lasted just over 30 minutes. The short list of songs included 'People Have The Power' and 'Walkin' Blind'.

The show was a form of rehearsal for the recording sessions for the follow-up to *Gone Again*, which resumed in a New York studio in mid-March. The sessions picked

up from where they had left off just before Christmas
1996, when approximately eight new songs had been laid
down. Most rumours and speculation suggested that the
album would be more of a rock album than *Gone Again*,
the main point of interest being that Patti was producing
the new album. Gossip-mongers pondered the reasons
for this move, since Lenny Kaye is an acclaimed record
producer (Soul Asylum, Kristin Hersh, Suzanne Vega)
and would now be returning to the functional role of
guitar-player. Patti clearly wanted complete control over
the record and wanted to extend her sphere of control to
include even the way it was recorded – which makes
perfect sense for an artist who signed her original recording contract with insistence on complete creative control.
It was also a wise career move, since she could start
producing other artists later on, as many artists do.

Peace And Noise, whose cover featured a stark black-
and-white portrait of Patti writing notes on a bed, taken
by Oliver Ray, was to ride a socially conscious theme,
tackle big issues, deliver hard rocking electric songs, music
that matched the message. Patti told *The Philadelphia
Enquirer* at the time of the album's release in October
1997 that the genesis of the record went back to discus-
sions she'd had with her late husband: "Fred and I spent
many hours discussing the kind of album we'd do after
Dream of Life. When he passed away I really didn't have
the heart to do that particular record. I focused on *Gone
Again* as a remembrance of Fred, but as I strengthened I
decided to continue the work we'd anticipated for
ourselves."

Most of the music for *Peace And Noise* was written by
Oliver Ray, who had first teamed up with Patti on *Gone*

Again. Very much arranged for a band, the album rocked in a way that harked back to the ragged, urgent sprawl of *Radio Ethiopia.* The songs were also predominantly cut live in a studio that had apparently once been a propeller factory. The sound reflected Patti's typical listening tastes of the time: The Grateful Dead, Nirvana, Bob Dylan, Beethoven and Jimi Hendrix, but the move back to Manhattan, where she had settled into a Soho loft with 15-year-old Jackson and 10-year-old Jesse, also inspired the return to an urban rock sound.

Where *Gone Again* had been a personal and raw wail of loss, *Peace And Noise* was a document of Patti returning to the city, turning 50, coming home to making music for an audience, looking around her at the world as it stood, feeling disturbed at what she saw. She told the *Austin Chronicle* in 2000 that the album emerged from a time and space when she was returning to music, her muse, coming back to her roots: "I was still getting my feet back on the ground and relearning how to record and perform myself, as everyone else was learning. We were learning to play together and getting to know each other as people."

The album opened with 'Waiting Underground', a Neil Young-esque dirge rocker, whose sombre piano recalls the glory days of *Easter.* Next up was 'Whirl Away', an assessment of global disharmony constructed on an itchy reggae guitar. The third track, '1959', an angry howl, spoke of the year the Chinese invaded Tibet (harking back to Patti's school project), the fate of the Tibetans and the Tibetan government in exile, a subject close to Patti's heart (she had recently performed at two New York-based Tibetan benefits: the Tibet-House

Benefit back in February and the Tibetan Freedom concert in June).

The album's stand-out track, 'Spell', brought that old Patti magic back, the poet and her immaculate recitation to the fore, as she drawls "Footnote to Howl" from beat poet Allen Ginsberg's 'Howl' over a haunting acoustic guitar motif and percussion and accompaniment with a North African flavour. The quoting of Ginsberg was Patti's tribute to the great poet who had passed away on April 5, 1997. In its mystical mood, 'Spell' was a step along from *Gone Again*'s 'Fireflies'; in lineage, the atmospherics went all the way back to the title track of *Wave*.

'Don't Say Nothing' kicks off with a funky keyboard shuffle before drifting into the melodic rocking pastures of *Dream Of Life*. 'Dead City' is pure retro CBGBs in sound, a slamming garage rock nugget, Patti's voice rawer, older, growling the blues over the top. 'Blue Poles', the first of two melancholy acoustic ballads, deals with the hardships that faced the Dust Bowl refugees and reminds the listener of *Gone Again*'s mournful themes.

Next up, 'Death Singing' features a teasing self-referential musical lift from 1978's 'We Three' from *Easter* and focuses on the tragedy of AIDS. The album's penultimate track, the 10-minute towering improvised sprawl of 'Memento Mori', features a furious resurrection of the song character Johnny from 1976's *Horses* cut, 'Land'. The album closes with 'Last Call', an eerie ballad about the Heaven's Gate cult mass suicide, which sees Michael Stipe making a guest appearance, returning the compliment of Patti lending her vocals to R.E.M.'s 'E-Bow The Letter'.

To promote the album, Patti appeared on the David

Letterman show and the Conan O'Brien show. At the end of October, she played an incendiary four-night residency at CBGBs in New York, completing a full career circle, airing the new songs at the legendary punk club she had risen from. At the start of November, she played to an invite-only mostly media audience at the Soho House club in London, before returning to the States to undertake a limited run of live dates in cities such as Providence, Boston, Washington D.C., Nashville and Atlanta. The tour was brief because of her commitments to her children and ended in North Carolina, a few days short of Christmas. By the end of 1997, *Peace And Noise* had reached its highest US album chart position of 152, a disappointment after *Gone Again*, which had peaked at 55.

Patti went into 1998 finishing work on a collection of notes and lyrics that would be published by Doubleday later the same year. It was a sign that Patti, who had previously fiercely guarded her creativity and privacy, was now prepared to grant fans access to the inner workings of her creative process. She again lent her support to the Tibetan cause, by performing at the Tibet-House benefit at the Carnegie Hall in March, at the Free Tibet concert on May 9 in Atlanta, Georgia and then the following day, also in Atlanta, as part of the live/cybercast A Flash Of Lightning: A Concert For The Dalai Lama.

Also in May, she read and performed at a memorial evening, titled A Tribute To Allen Ginsberg, held at the Cathedral of St John the Divine in New York. The following month, poetry was still on her mind, when she flew out to Granada, Spain, with Oliver Ray to perform what she billed as a 'reading with guitars' at the event,

Lorca And Popular Music: A Centenary Celebration. By midsummer, she performed a residency at the Bowery Ballroom over four nights, from July 28–31 and at the start of August, she was back in Europe, to play four festival dates in Salzburg, Vienna, Budapest and Dranouter. After that, she flew back to the US to play three California dates, before heading off to play a short tour in Australia and New Zealand.

In October 1998, Doubleday published *Patti Smith Complete: Lyrics, Reflections & Notes For The Future* and it was, as promised, a select gathering of her song lyrics and other notes. The book appeared in hardback at first and was then published as a paperback the following year. To promote the book, Patti embarked on a US tour which lasted until the end of the year, when she played the Bowery Ballroom on December 30 and then New Year's Eve, which featured all-star surprise guest appearances from Michael Stipe, Thurston Moore, Kim Gordon and guitar from Patti's son, Jackson.

She went into 1999, as before, performing at the annual Tibet-House benefit, which was held in February, again at the Carnegie Hall. As with 1998, there was no new studio album on the cards. The focus of the year would be further touring: getting her message and music to as broad an audience as possible. Much of 1999 had a gypsy feel to it, as Patti played far and wide. In the early part of the year, she played New York, Venice, Brussels and Amsterdam, before appearing at the Glastonbury Festival in the UK in June. After that, she played Dublin, Manchester, London and Brighton, before crossing the Channel to perform in Paris and Vienna. By July, she was heading East on her travels, playing dates in Istanbul,

Turkey and Thessalonika, Greece, before heading to a cluster of dates in Italy, then back east again to perform in Tel Aviv, Israel.

She was back in the US for two shows in early September before taking herself off the road until the end of the year, when she once more played the Bowery Ballroom on December 30 and New Year's Eve. The emphasis on touring was a way of keening her edge, re-finding herself, merging past and present. She told the *Berkshire Eagle* in 2000 why playing live was so important to her: "Every night is different and the course of the night is different. That's one of the things that makes performing for me so wonderful and difficult. Our band really strives to reach whatever heights we can but also be aware that we are in the present and also that we are amongst our people and we're not playing at the people. We're not just entertaining a faceless crowd. We're trying to have some kind of communication, some kind of meaningful exchange with the people."

Patti entered 2000 with an amazing new studio album ready to launch. The two years of hard touring had shaped the band, lent their community and sound an immense and intense bond. She unveiled some of the new material at a show at the Bowery Ballroom in February 2000. Like *Peace And Noise*, the emphasis was on hard nosed guitar based rock music. The new album, *Gung Ho*, was produced by Gil Norton, best known for producing Boston based American band The Pixies. His touch lent the album a fullness and a polish missing from *Peace And Noise* and *Gone Again*. The no-frills approach was replaced respectfully by more sheen, more layering, adding depth.

Gung Ho was released in March 2000. The cover image

was a photograph of Patti's father, who had passed away in August 1999, taken in Australia when he was serving in the army during the Second World War. The title alluded to the title track which looked at the life and times of Ho Chi Minh, as well as to Gunga Din, whose life also interested Patti. She told *The Austin Chronicle* in 2000: "My mother always used to use that term, gung-ho. It was used for someone who was putting their whole heart into something and really believing in what they were doing and even going into a difficult task with positive, idealistic energy. I decided that I wanted to enter the new century like that. We have so many things that are wrong, so many difficult things. I wanted to go into the new century in a positive, work oriented frame of mind."

The album opens with the folksy sea shanty sway of 'One Voice', a slick tribute to Mother Teresa's charitable life and work (Patti had appeared at the event Mother Teresa, One Voice, on New Year's Day in New York). The second track, 'Lo And Beholden', returns to the classic melodic feel of *Easter*, the song both melancholic and uplifting. Singing from the perspective of Biblical character Salome, Patti uses the beautiful girl's fall from grace after dancing the dance of the seven veils to help her mother take the head of John The Baptist, as a way to look at, as Patti put it to *The Austin Chronicle* in 2000, the way in which society today is "exploiting youth and beauty these days. Girls are being exploited terribly."

'Boy Cried Wolf' is a mid-tempo Dylan-esque track which wouldn't sound out of place on *Dream Of Life*. 'Persuasion' was originally written by Fred Smith for *Dream Of Life* but the track didn't fit the body of work that eventually made up that earlier album. Patti revisited the song for *Gung Ho* and it was Oliver Ray's idea that Patti's son, Jackson, by now 17, stand in Fred's shoes for the guitar solo. 'Gone Pie' is a taut mid-tempo rock track, driven by an angular guitar riff. The mournful ballad 'China Bird', very reminiscent of the sound and mood of *Easter* and *Wave*, is a hymn to her deceased father.

'Glitter In Their Eyes', a hard rocking cut, looks at the way young people are targeted and lured by consumerism. It features guest appearances by Michael Stipe and Television guitarist Tom Verlaine. 'Strange Messengers' has a haunted Led Zeppelin feel, Patti's voice and the band creating an eerie landscape. The minor chord ballad 'Grateful', which Patti wrote on an acoustic guitar, was inspired by The Grateful Dead's Jerry Garcia.

'Upright Come' is another jaunty fist-in-the-air call to activism, the kind of track that Patti has always leaned towards. After that comes the funk-rock sludge of 'New Party', a track that bears the distinct influence of the Red Hot Chili Peppers. Penultimate track 'Libby's Song' is a lovely old folk ballad, the perfect form for Patti's voice and then the album closes with the aforementioned 'Gung Ho', this record's 'Memento Mori', a lengthy mesmerising, improvised track that explores Ho Chi Minh's life and his legacy on Vietnamese history.

She promoted the record with appearances on the Charlie Rose show, the David Letterman show and *Tonight With Jay Leno*. Patti also went out on tour again, playing a lengthy US/Canadian tour which started in March and ran on until the end of July. Meanwhile, despite positive reviews, *Gung Ho* peaked on the US *Billboard* album chart at 178, a lower placing than *Peace And Noise*, which reached 152, a disappointment for all concerned, since the intensive touring between records should have expanded her audience and, as a result, led to increased sales.

In the fall of 2000, Patti played live in support of Ralph Nader, who was running for President as the candidate for the Green Party of The United States. She performed at the Ralph Nader Rally and Benefit at Madison Square Garden on October 13, at another rally at the Kaiser Stadium in Oakland, California, on October 21 and at CGBGs on November 1. Further dates followed with Patti performing in Amsterdam and then arriving in the UK for Patti Smith, A Solo Performance: Song & Spoken Word: In Honour Of William Blake at St James' Church, Piccadilly, in London's West End. After a date at the Stone Pony club in Asbury Park, New Jersey on December 29, the year ended in what by now had become a Patti Smith New Year's tradition, with a pair of dates at the Bowery Ballroom in New York on December 30 and 31.

At the beginning of 2001, the beat poet Gregory Corso died, another death in the artistic community which hit Patti hard. She performed at his funeral on January 24 in New York and again at events celebrating his life in March and April. In February, she honoured another annual commitment and appeared at the Tibet-House benefit.

On May 1, 2001 she set out on the road again, her commitment to the road starting to seem somewhat Bob Dylan-esque in its gypsy regularity. The tour tracked the East Coast and ended June 10 at the Bardavon Opera house in Poughkeepsie, New York. After that, Patti and band headed over to Europe to play the Roskilde Festival in Denmark, before going on to take in dates in Vienna,

Ljubljana, Prague, Paris, Florence, Montreux, Turin, Catania, Rome and Ostend. Then they went over to the UK to play two dates, in late July, at the Ocean in London. From there, it was on to Japan and Hawaii before heading back to the US in August to play dates which started on the West Coast in Seattle, went down to San Francisco, up to Chicago and then over to New York for a final date in late August.

By October, Patti was playing further dates, including another Ralph Nader rally in November in Boston. Then it was back to Europe to play the Numero Festival in Lisbon on December 1. Again, she ended the year with a date at the Stone Pony club in Asbury Park, New Jersey, before returning to New York to see the year out with the usual pair of dates at the Bowery Ballroom on December 30 and New Year's Eve.

2002 began with a reading on the first day of the New Year at The Poetry Project at St Mark's Church in New York, something Patti had also done on January 1 in 2000 and 2001. At the end of January, she performed at another Ralph Nader rally, this one in Austin, Texas. Mid-February, Patti played a series of dates in Spain and Italy, before returning to the US to honour another annual tradition – appearing at the Tibet-House benefit.

That spring, Patti and Arista, her label of 27 years, parted company. The final release was *Land (1975–2002)*, a two disc compilation offering a 'best of' on one disc and a rarities compilation on the other. To promote the album, Patti went on the David Letterman show at the beginning of April and performed 'Dancing Barefoot', the classic track from *Wave* often covered by U2. The 'best of' featured a bonus cover of Prince's 'When Doves

Cry'. She then undertook dates in Atlanta, Georgia and Tampa, Florida, before heading back to play in Italy, then travelling to London to play 'Because The Night' and 'Dancing Barefoot' on the BBC *Later With Jools Holland* show. Various appearances followed, before Patti again lent her support to a Ralph Nader rally on June 29 in Portland, Oregon.

Cut loose from the label and with the retrospective to push, Patti's increasingly demanding touring schedule raged on, taking in a series of dates in Japan in July, a mini-tour of the UK in August, before a run of shows in Belgium, Germany, Poland, Austria and Switzerland. Back in the US she performed in support of Patriots For Peace And Social Justice on September 11, 2002 and played at an anti-(Iraq/Afghanistan) war rally in Washington DC in October.

After a brief period of uncertainty without a recording contract, Patti signed a new deal with Columbia Records on October 20, 2002. She spoke of her joy at joining a label synonymous with Bob Dylan and Miles Davis and of the creative freedom the new deal afforded her. On a high, she closed the year as she had for several years now, by playing the Stone Pony club in Asbury Park, New Jersey, on December 28 and then heading back to New York for a three night residency at the Bowery Ballroom between December 29 and 31.

2003 started, as per recent routine, with an appearance at the Poetry Project at St Mark's Church in New York. It would be another significant year in terms of live performance but also a year that moved towards the creation of her debut album for Columbia Records, *Trampin'*. She played a handful of US dates during the early part of the year, including another Ralph Nader rally in Tampa, Florida, in April.

On May 9, she was in Scotland to appear at the Burns An' A' That Festival, part of her ongoing commitment to the literary thread of her interests and career. She then appeared at the Cathedral Quarter Arts Festival in Belfast and, after that, at the Charleston Festival in Sussex, where Patti read excerpts from Virginia Woolf's *The Waves*, as well as a selection of her own work. She returned to the US to play a handful of East and West Coast shows, before taking off for another mini-tour of Japan in July, before heading from there to play dates in Italy, Switzerland, Hungary, Austria, Denmark, Germany, France and lastly, London, in mid-August.

During autumn of 2003, the new album, *Trampin'*, was recorded at Loho Studio in New York City with Patti and band producing. By October, she was ready to test-run new material with a pair of dates in Philadelphia and three further dates in Italy. On December 19 the exhibition *Strange Messenger: The Work Of Patti Smith* opened at the Haus Der Kunst gallery in Munich, Germany. The exhibit, which would end on February 29, 2004, included over 100 works on paper by Patti, including a new series of large-scale drawings inspired by the 9/11 terrorist attacks. The show also included original manuscripts, photographs and the video *Summer Cannibals*, by photographer Robert Frank. The exhibition was complemented by a homage to Patti in the form of works by fashion designer Ann Demeulemeester, inspired by Patti's *Wool Gathering* book. Patti flew over to Germany for the opening of the exhibit and played a date in Dresden, before performing at the opening night of the exhibition on December 19. This year ended with Patti playing her usual residency at the Bowery Ballroom on December 29, 30 and 31.

2004 began, as per pattern, with a reading at The Poetry Project at St Mark's Church in New York. There was excitement in the air too, about her debut for Sony Columbia. New label, new terms, new deal. Advance hype said it was a new era for Patti, an album made free of creative limitations and restrictions.

In February she played the Tibet-House benefit in New York and then headed over to Europe to play shows in London, Ferrara, Paris, Brussels and Berlin before returning to headline the charitable event Peaceable Kingdom With Patti Smith And Friends, held at the Cathedral Church of St-John the Divine in New York, in support of The Parents Circle who describe themselves as "a bi-national organisation formed in 1995 by Yitzhak Frankenthal after the murder of his son by Hamas in 1994". The organisation has since expanded, gathering support. They describe their purpose as follows: "Today over 200 Israeli and Palestinian families who have lost a loved one in the conflict, belong to the circle. The group offers support and encouragement among its members, both Israeli and Palestinian, who have paid the ultimate price, share the same pain and sense of loss. Together, they serve each other as sources of strength and pursue their common interest in promoting peace and reconciliation in the volatile region through education, negotiation, meetings with influential world leaders, lectures and summer camps."

On April 16 Patti aired 'Jubilee', a track from her new album, on the David Letterman show. Eleven days later, on April 27, 2004, *Trampin'* was released to universal acclaim. The cover featured a stark black-and-white image of Patti's foot floating above the earth, in the midst of journey, shot by Melodie McDaniel.

Patti summarised the mood of the album when talking to *Uncut* magazine, saying: "It's been a long road and I'm still walking on it. I think the idea is like the Pilgrim's Progress or something. Life indeed takes us on what journeys it takes us on. It takes us to a lot of places we hadn't anticipated. I think the record unfolds as much as life does."

The album opens with 'Jubilee', an exuberant stomp, a classic in a long line of classic calls to arms in the Patti Smith canon. She told *Uncut* what inspired the song: "'Jubilee', as it unfolded, turned out to speak of my country at the present time. It's the point of view of a mother or a woman or a strong person who is extolling the beauty of the land and the optimism and the young spirit of her country but also the fact that there's trouble brewing right now, there's things that are not right. Our present administration has put our country in a very rough position financially and environmentally and, I think, psychologically." She was talking, of course, about President George W. Bush and his government's foreign policy, notably in Iraq and Afghanistan.

The second track, 'Mother Rose', is a pretty, sad but uplifting slow-tempo ballad, which Patti penned for her mother, who had recently passed away. Unlike many of the grief stricken songs on *Gone Again*, Patti told *Uncut*: "It's more of a thank you to her and also hopefully a really pretty song. It's not a grieving song."

'Stride Of The Mind' has a low-slung riff that wouldn't

sound out of place on a Blue Öyster Cult album. The vocal delivery is reminiscent of many performances on *Wave*. The fourth track, 'Cartwheels', built on a Doorsy hypnotic, swirling guitar motif, is another of Patti's mystical works, an otherworldly song. The monumental, lengthy 'Gandhi' is the latest of Patti's leader/hero/ heroine inspiration hymns. After looking over the years at so many inspiring figures and artists and legends, Patti was now turning her attentions to India's great spiritual and social figurehead: Mahatma Gandhi – an expected development in light of her recent reverence for similar-minded individuals such as the Dalai Lama and Mother Teresa.

'Trespasses' is a stark acoustic folk ballad, the second-loveliest track on *Trampin'*. It's another song preoccupied with the spectre of death, the facts of loss. She told *Uncut* though that the song is about acceptance of death, not endless mourning: "Sometimes I can feel my brother in my heart, he always made me laugh. So y'know I have my own internal universe in the way that I deal with these things and I find that it's much more helpful than being stricken, grief stricken, month after month, year after year, because you can't be productive and you can't conduct yourself in the way that people that you lose and who loved you would like to see you conduct yourself. There's a song on the album called 'Trespasses' and at the end the father obviously dies, the mother dies and the son at the end takes up their deaths and takes up everything and the last line is he takes up this ragged coat, the symbol of their deaths and all the things done and left undone in their lives, whistling joyfully."

'My Blakean Year', which rides a dampened slick

guitar sound (rather like many tracks on *Dream Of Life*) inevitably grew out of Patti's involvement with the William Blake event in London. The song 'Cash' passes wistfully, with a melancholy undercurrent. Her voice sounds fabulous on 'Peaceable Kingdom', a call for world peace, sung over another classic sad/uplifting musical backing, the kind we've been hearing from Patti since *Horses*. The penultimate track, 'Radio Baghdad', makes no bones about its subject matter (the war in Iraq) and weaves a kind of Doors' 'Riders On The Storm' atmosphere to hard jagged rock in the vein of Led Zeppelin's *Physical Graffitti* album.

The album's closer is the beauty on this record, simply quite luminous. 'Trampin'', the title track, is a traditional gospel song, featuring piano from Patti's daughter, Jesse. Tender, fragile, timeless: it's a goosebumps affair, Patti singing from the heart about her endless quest to find a comfortable spiritual place in this world. She said of the song's coming alive to *Uncut*: "I like Marian Anderson and I have a little space where I paint and take photographs and I often listen to gospel records and spirituals. That little song, for the past couple of years, has always attracted me, and I asked my daughter if she would learn it on piano. That's my daughter playing and it's live, we just did it a couple of times and took one that was honest." Of the song's subject matter she explained: "It does have a weary quality but it's optimistic. This person is trampin' trying to find Heaven, they're not just trying to get to the corner store or just trying to get to a soup kitchen, they're going for the highest place. I like the little song and there's a lot of miles tramped in this album and I think it was a good way to end it."

To set the album off on its journey, Patti played a four-night residency at the Warsaw club in Brooklyn over the first four nights of May 2004, which then segued into a significant US tour. By the end of June, she had started a brief UK tour, taking in dates in Birmingham, Edinburgh, Manchester and London, before crossing to mainland Europe to play various headlining dates and festivals in France, Germany, Belgium, Norway, Sweden, Switzerland, Spain and Italy, over the summer. By August 12, she was back in the US for a month of West Coast dates that also took in a show in Vancouver. At the end of September, she played two dates in Italy, then returned once more to play a handful of US East Coast shows including the American Civil Liberties Union Freedom Concert at Avery Fisher Hall in New York. She played extensive dates in France and Italy throughout October, before wrapping the year up with a half dozen East Coast US shows, including the by now traditional three night residency at the Bowery Ballroom in New York over December 29, 30 and New Year's Eve. And so the year ended with Patti very much back at the top of her game, with *Trampin'* having peaked on the US album chart at 123, a much higher placing that *Gung Ho*, bringing Patti her best record sales since *Gone Again*.

12

Patti The Icon

THE year 2005 began as was now routine with a reading at The Poetry Project at St Mark's Church in New York. Following that, the early quarter of the year was devoted to Patti's cries for a better and more peaceful world. The more she talked of the inspiration she found in Gandhi, Mother Teresa and Jesus Christ, the more she turned her sights on what she could do to inform people about issues she considered important; what she could do to pressure issues herself. From January through to April, she performed at numerous Stop the Iraq War rallies; at a less specific anti-war rally; at a Tibet House benefit; and at a show in support of Ralph Nader.

In the summer, she headed to London where she had agreed to curate the latest in the series of annual Melt-down Festivals at the South Bank Centre. The festival organisers chose Patti in celebration of it being the thirtieth anniversary of the release of *Horses*.

Patti rose to the challenge and picked an eclectic array of artists to appear including Rachid Taha, Antony & The Johnsons, Steve Earle, Television, Yoko Ono, Beth Orton, Marc Almond, Eels, Johnny Marr, Joanna Newsom, Martha Wainwright, Brian Jonestown Massacre,

Billy Bragg, Richard Hell, Sinead O'Connor and John Cale. Certain performances were curated around celebrations of artists she revered – William Blake, Bertold Brecht, William S. Burroughs and Jimi Hendrix.

One highlight of the festival was a night in tribute of Robert Mapplethorpe, at which Patti read the entirety of *The Coral Sea*, set to music by My Bloody Valentine's sound-manipulating maestro Kevin Shields. The other highlight was a night when Patti performed *Horses* in its entirety.

The night re-creating *Horses* sold out almost as soon as tickets went on sale. Patti told *The Observer* how she felt when she heard: "I was overwhelmed. To tell the truth, it brought tears to my eyes. *Horses* pretty much broke as a record in England. I always think of us as a semi-English band because we were so maverick in America and then we went to London and played that first date at the Roundhouse in May 1976 and the response gave me my first sense that, wow, we're really doing something."

The performance of *Horses* was so successful that Arista would release a new edition entitled *Horses/Horses* in November 2005, the first disc featuring a remastered version of the original studio album, the second disc offering a live recording of the re-staging of the album at the Meltdown Festival. The album was released to coincide with the actual thirtieth anniversary of its original release.

After the success of the Meltdown Festival, Patti took off for dates in Italy at the end of June and then spent the rest of summer on the road, playing dates and festivals in Spain, France, Greece, New York, the UK, Belgium, the Netherlands, Germany, Austria, Denmark, the Czech

Republic, Finland, Russia and Iceland.

During that leg of touring, on July 10, 2005, Patti's life-long work was honoured with a prestigious award in France. She was named a Commander of the Ordre des Arts et des Lettres by the French Culture Ministry. The award was given to her by the Minister of Culture, Renaud Donnedieu de Vabres, who noted her influential role in rock'n'roll history, as well as her tireless celebration of the work of French poet Arthur Rimbaud.

As September became October, Patti's endless globe trotting continued, as more dates rolled by in the US as well as in Belgium, Italy and France. In November, she opened both of U2's headline shows at Madison Square Garden and joined long-time fan of hers, Bono, during U2's set on November 21, to sing a duet of John Lennon's 'Instant Karma'.

On October 11, Patti published a new work of poetry called *Auguries Of Innocence*. It was her first work of poetry in a decade – the last having been *The Coral Sea*. Published by Ecco press, an imprint of Harper Collins, it featured 26 poems, many wearing the influence of William Blake, as implied by the collection being named after Blake's poem of the same title. As ever, influences were celebrated within the poems, with Patti referencing the likes of Virginia Woolf, Arthur Rimbaud, Pablo Picasso, Diane Arbus and Joan of Arc. The collection's centrepiece is 'Birds of Iraq', a terse poem about the US invasion of Iraq.

In late November and early December, Patti played a variety of shows in the Netherlands and in New York, before concluding 2005 with a pair of shows, on December 30 and 31, at the Bowery Ballroom in New York.

She entered 2006 performing at The Poetry Project at St Mark's Church in New York. Later that month, she flew out to Austria where she spent a week taking part in artist, actor and director Christoph Schlingensief's installation project Area 7 – Matthäusexpedition.

On February 11, she performed at a memorial service for Ralph Nader's mother Rose at St James Episcopal Church in Winsted, Connecticut and then, after stopping in Italy for a show in Milan, she flew out to Dakar, Senegal, for the Football For Africa concert on March 1.

Late March, she was back in Vienna, continuing her involvement with Area 7, an ongoing affair that culminated on May 6, when Patti played the 'closing sequence' to the exhibition. Around this commitment, she also performed in New York, Glasgow and Ireland.

On May 25, she was in the UK to appear at the Charleston Festival and also to open her exhibition of photographs, titled Moments of Being, at the Charleston Gallery. The photographs mostly harked back to summer 2003, when Patti had briefly been in residence at Charleston House, where she spent time contemplating the Bloomsbury Set legacy, notably that of Virginia Woolf. The photographs were mostly of the local area and one, especially haunting, was of the River Ouse, in which Woolf tragically drowned herself.

The rest of summer she played further shows, in California, New Jersey, France, Sweden and the UK (the Latitude Festival and a surprise appearance duetting on 'Hey Joe' with the Red Hot Chili Peppers in London) before heading back to the US to appear at the Lollapolooza Festival in Chicago.

In September Patti was back in London, for a season

of events in memory of Robert Mapplethorpe. On September 8, she performed at an evening titled Robert Mapplethorpe: Words And Music at the Tate Modern gallery. Then over two nights, September 11 and 12, she again collaborated with My Bloody Valentine's Kevin Shields, on The Coral Sea Sessions: An Evening Of Poetry and Music In Remembrance Of Robert Mapplethorpe, which was staged at the Queen Elizabeth Hall on London's South Bank.

On September 9, two days ahead of the performances with Kevin Shields, *The Independent* newspaper, under the headline 'Patti Smith rails against Israel and US', told readers that Patti would be premiering two new songs at her South Bank shows: "The American singer takes the Israeli bombing of Lebanese civilians and the US detention centre at Guantanamo Bay as her subjects in the songs 'Qana' and 'Without Chains'." The article went on to quote Patti about her reasons for writing the songs, "I wrote both these songs directly in response to events that I felt outraged about. These are injustices against children and the young men and women who are being incarcerated. I'm an American, I pay taxes in my name and they are giving millions and millions of dollars to a country such as Israel and cluster bombs and defence technology and those bombs were dropped on common citizens in Qana. It's terrible. It's a human rights violation." Despite such strong statement, *The Independent* reported that Patti did not get into specific discussion of that summer's Israel-Lebanon war: "Smith said she was not sufficiently well versed in Middle East politics to discuss the differences between Israel and Lebanon."

The first of the two dates, on September 11, was

reviewed in *The Guardian*, whose correspondent noted the poignancy of the date: "The evening starts by marking the fifth anniversary of 9/11. As footage shot by a friend of Manhattan on the day of the attacks is screened, Smith intones the number killed in those attacks, before going on to invoke the far higher toll exacted by the subsequent 'war on terror', and launches into an elegiac clarinet solo."

Back in New York City, after Hilly Kristal lost his battle to maintain the lease and keep CBGBs open, the club threw a final-night party on October 15, at which Patti and band performed for three and a half hours. The BBC quoted Patti as saying during the show, "We can have CBGB in our hearts, but the new generation is going to have their own places to play. They're going to find some shit hole and play in it like we did." *Billboard* reviewed the show, which featured Patti, Lenny Kaye, Jay Dee and Tony Shanahan, and guest appearances by Flea and Television guitarist Richard Lloyd. "Smith remained focused and upbeat throughout the majority of her performance," read the review, "but became emotional at show's end as she read a list of names of deceased figures who had played a prominent role in the club's history – like Joey, Johnny and Dee Dee Ramone, Johnny Thunders and her own former bandmate Richard Sohl – and then shouted out a teary, emphatic thank you to CBs owner Hilly Kristal."

In November 2006, an exhibition opened at the Trolley Gallery titled Sur Les Traces. The exhibition featured polaroids taken by Patti and ran until January 2007. The show was a fund raiser to help finance the printing and publishing of a book about the summer 2006

Israel–Lebanon war called *Double Blind*, featuring photographs by Paolo Pellegrin, who was reporting on the ground in Lebanon during the conflict for *Newsweek* and *The New York Times*.

As the exhibition was on, Patti was busy performing in Brazil, Argentina and the UK. Her year ended with a triple night residency at the Bowery Ballroom.

2007 got underway with the now traditional appearance at The Poetry Project at St Mark's where Patti performed 'Qana'. Ten days later, she made a brief appearance with Lenny Kaye, singing and reading at the Robert Miller Gallery in New York. The rest of the month passed with two further low key New York performances.

At the start of February, Columbia announced that on April 7 it would release a new Patti album called *Twelve* which would feature a set of twelve cover versions. The album was timely since Patti was about to step up from rock idol status to rock icon status in March, when she was to be inducted into the Rock 'n' Roll Hall of Fame.

A run of dates, starting in Boston on February 21, ended with another performance at the Tibet House Benefit concert, held at Carnegie Hall. Her performance at the benefit included a cover of R.E.M.'s 'Everybody Hurts', which she sang with Michael Stipe.

On March 12, Patti joined the Rock 'n' Roll Hall of Fame along with R.E.M., Van Halen, The Ronettes and Grandmaster Flash & The Furious Five. The ceremony was held at the Waldorf Astoria Hotel and she was inducted by Rage Against The Machine's Zack de la Rocha who honoured her with a moving, eloquent speech.

And then on April 17, *Twelve* was released. The album offered cover versions of a dozen classics including The Rolling Stones' 'Gimme Shelter', Jimi Hendrix's 'Are You Experienced?', Paul Simon's 'The Boy In The Bubble', Nirvana's 'Smells Like Teen Spirit', and The Beatles' 'Within You, Without You'. The track selection seemed rather unimaginative – the kind of list an amateur covers band might choose to play in a provincial bar on a Saturday night: a bit of something for everyone, every track recognisable, as if selected from a jukebox.

Reviewers were divided about the album. *Pitchfork*'s reviewer called it "shockingly conservative" and pondered its purpose: "of course Smith loves 'Gimme Shelter' – who doesn't? But why would anyone reach for Smith's version over the Stones', especially when Smith brings nothing new to a song whose original performance still drips with danger, menace and mystery?"

Spin magazine's reviewer didn't see the purpose either, writing: "Patti Smith misplaces her fearless edge on this oddly subdued set of covers. Versions of Nirvana's 'Smells Like Teen Spirit' and the Stones' 'Gimme Shelter' add nothing to the perfect originals." Other reviewers, however, loved the album. A review in *The Guardian* called *Twelve* an "entertaining sweep through the rock canon that Smith has eloquently championed down the years".

No matter how divisive, fans voted with their wallets and the album reached a high on the *Billboard* album chart of 60, Patti's best position in several albums.

With the Rock 'n' Roll Hall of Fame nomination followed by a solid chart position, Patti was now officially a rock icon. The canonisation complete, she could now run with the mythology.

A flurry of New York-area dates in April segued into a pair of Los Angeles dates before Patti flew to Europe. A lengthy European tour started on May 10 and continued all the way until mid July, when she played a final date in Milan, Italy, before heading back to the US.

Once home, she played a show in Cleveland at the end of the month, before taking off on a US tour which lasted until August 16. Further US shows in September book-ended shows in Greece and also in Turkey. Patti was touring *Twelve* hard and firmly back in the limelight.

For the rest of the year, she stayed on the road, playing shows in Canada and the US as well as taking a second run at the UK and France, and also performing in Portugal and the Netherlands. In November, Random House published an anthology of William Blake's poetry, per-sonally selected by Patti. She also wrote an introduction to the book – another homage realised. She returned to New York from Europe to end 2007 on a triumphant note with a three night residency at the Bowery Ballroom on December 29–31.

As per usual, Patti launched 2008 at St Mark's Church. Several weeks later, she was in Utah for the Sundance Film Festival, where Steven Sebring's documentary, *Patti Smith: Dream Of Life*, premiered. The film was reviewed by *Variety*, which described it as follows: "The result of 11 years of filming (much of it in wonderfully grainy black-and-white 16 mm), pic is designed as a stream-of-consciousness experience, following Smith as she revives her music career and considers every aspect of her life."

Dates in Germany, Spain and France kept Patti on European soil during February and March, before she touched down in Paris for the opening of her major solo exhibition Land 250 at the Fondation Cartier de l'art Contemporain. The show, named after the Land 250 polaroid camera, ran from March 28 to June 22 and celebrated Patti's visual work – her photographs, found objects, mementos, drawings, writings.

The *Daily Telegraph* described the exhibition as being "at once a showcase for Smith's Polaroid photographs, a kind of career retrospective, and an interactive tour of her New York home and psyche". Speaking with the newspaper, Patti explained why the show meant so much to her, "It's an amazing story for me, because I came here in May, I think, of 1969 with my sister Linda. I used to tell my sister – I was so arrogant – 'I'm going to be a great artist some day and I'm going to have a big show in Paris, even though we don't have enough money to eat. Someday, you know, we'll be eating caviar.' You know, it took 40 years, but the beautiful thing is my sister is such a humble, sweet, hard-working girl and I am going to bring her to one of the best hotels in Paris."

To accompany the exhibition, Fondation Cartier published a 272-page monograph titled *Land 250*, featuring 250 black-and-white photographs by Patti, as well as anecdotally fascinating captions throughout. Fondation Cartier also published a three-book set titled *Trois*, which consists of three artist's books: *Charleville*, *Photographies* and *Cahier*. *Charleville*, where Arthur Rimbaud is buried, centres on Patti's lifelong infatuation with the French poet and offered souvenir documents from her 1973 pilgrimage to Charleville in search of the Rimbaud legend. *Photographies* collects select Patti photographs. *Cahier* begins but then stops on page five, with the note 'Ces pages sont a vous', meaning 'these pages are for you':

turning the rest of the notebook over to whoever pur-
chased that copy. Both publications were published
outside of France by Thames & Hudson.

During the exhibition, Patti was often in Europe,
playing intermittent shows in the UK, France, Spain,
Norway and Italy.

In July, a double live album was released by independent label, PASK, celebrating Patti's performances back
in 2005 and 2006, of *The Coral Sea*, with My Bloody
Valentine's Kevin Shields.

That month, Patti kept on touring, her iconic status
growing, as she hit the summer festivals circuit, appearing
in Lebanon, Greece, Italy, Norway, Sweden, Spain,
before returning to play a scattering of New York shows
in August.

At the end of August, she played the first of four dates
in Russia, opening another new front in her global campaign. She stayed on the road for the rest of 2008, playing
dates in the US, Australia, France, Denmark, Spain,
Germany, showing no signs of slowing down. The year
ended with the now expected three night residency at the
Bowery Ballroom.

Patti began 2009 performing at St Mark's Church,
before going on to repeat the formula of recent years:
which is to say, it was another year on the road, Bob
Dylan eternal gypsy style. During the first half of the year,
Patti's touring concentrated on the US and Italy. Then, in
June, Patti played a cluster of shows in the UK including
the Meltdown Festival, curated this year by Ornette
Coleman. After that, she again concentrated on the
summer festivals, which saw her perform in Italy, Croatia,
Serbia, Austria, Germany, Slovakia, before taking off for

Japan. A handful of US shows in August were followed by another tour of Italy.

Mid October, she was back in London to perform a small show in celebration of an opening of a Robert Mapplethorpe exhibition at the Alison Jacques gallery. After that, she returned to the US, playing a series of shows, which climaxed in a three-night residency at the end of the year at the Bowery Ballroom.

2010 began with a performance at St Mark's Church and then became all about a new book by Patti – a memoir – called *Just Kids*. The intimate, beautifully written book, Patti's first work of prose, spoke of the early years of her relationship with Robert Mapplethorpe and was published by Harper Collins' imprint, Ecco Press, on January 19, to instant, universal acclaim. To promote it and build on the glowing reviews, Patti set out on an extensive reading tour across the US and UK, which took the form of either readings or readings combined with music.

In May, Patti was given an honorary doctorate in Fine Arts by the Pratt Institute, along with writer Jonathan Lethem, filmmaker Steven Soderbergh and architect Daniel Libeskind.

By June, Patti and band were back on the road, once more tearing up the summer festivals circuit. In October, she was in France to promote the French edition of *Just Kids*, giving readings in Paris and Strasbourg.

On November 17 yet further acclaim came to Patti when *Just Kids* won the prestigious National Book Award for Nonfiction. The award sparked another round of promotion for the book, taking Patti to the end of 2010, which she closed, as usual, with the three-night residency at the Bowery Ballroom.

2011 began with Patti performing at St Mark's Church. She was starting the year on a tremendous high, the last four years having been a rush of newfound infamy and success. Her iconic status was sealed now, completely.

Constantly on the road, promoting *Just Kids* or touring her music, Patti travelled to Europe, for events in Paris, London, Vienna, Rome and Geneva.

On May 3, 2011, Patti was co-awarded the Polar Music Prize, a prestigious Swedish music prize, which she shared with the Kronos Quartet. The prize was presented to her by Swedish writer Henning Mankell who, in his prize citation, described Patti as a "Rimbaud with Marshall amps".

On June 26, Patti fans were surprised to see her on TV guesting on a new episode of the popular drama *Law & Order: Criminal Intent*. In an episode titled 'Icarus', Patti appeared as a university mythology professor who offers her expert knowledge of the myth of Icarus, helping detectives Eames and Goren solve a case about a Broadway actor who dies while performing a stunt onstage.

That summer, Patti was busy with the festival circuit again, performing in Norway, Germany, the Netherlands, the UK and the US.

On August 23, Sony released *Outside Society*, an 18-track single volume 'greatest hits' compilation. The career encompassing album was designed to build on *Just Kids*' success and introduce newcomers who had discovered Patti via the book to her rich musical legacy.

On September 7, Patti had a new exhibition, titled Patti Smith: 9.11 Babelogue, open at the Bertha & Karl Leubsdorf Art Gallery, Hunter College, in New York. Patti showed 26 works on paper, each created in response to the 9/11 terrorist attacks on the World Trade Center. The exhibition would run until the beginning of December.

On September 8, she performed a free concert organised by French Inter, the French National Public Radio Channel, at Webster Hall, commemorating the tenth anniversary of the Twin Towers attacks.

By the end of September, Patti was still receiving rave reviews for *Outside Society*. The album had introduced a new audience to her music and built on the glow of success brought on by *Just Kids'* tremendous reception. Now 64, approaching 65, Patti was firmly up there, for good, with Mick Jagger, Lou Reed, Keith Richards, Paul McCartney, Bob Dylan, David Bowie and all the rock greats who have persisted and endured. She plays to sell-out audiences all over the world. She has a bestselling book to her name and many critically acclaimed works of poetry in her back catalogue. The list of artists who cite her as a primary influence gets longer every day; just as the list of artists and figures who have influenced Patti and continue to influence Patti gets longer every day. Since her troubled and painful comeback in the mid-nineties, she has fought her way back to the top. And her myth will only grow larger via her furious work ethic.

At one point during the early stages of writing the original version of this book, back in 1996, when I was attempting to find out if Patti would grant me a series of interviews or collaborate with me, one of her representatives explained that Patti had been chewing over a fax I had sent. The representative came back a few weeks later and told me that Patti felt it was too early in her career for a serious book to be written about her work. She had too many plans and was sure her best work was still to come. Initially, I thought this was a case of modesty gone mad, but then realised that Patti Smith would inevitably go on to create enough new art to warrant the writing of a sequel to this book in a decade or two. And I was right: and here it is: the updated 'sequel' to the original book, 15 years later, at a time when Patti is even bigger than she was back then: no longer a rock idol; but a rock icon and more than that, one of the great American artists of our time.

Once more, I walk along the third avenue transversale in Père-Lachaise cemetery. There is nobody in sight; it's a crisp silent morning. I check the cemetery guide and know that I'm close. To find the grave I'm looking for, I have to come off the official path and enter the network of headstones and memorial crypts. Soil is sticking to my shoes; names and dates are demanding my attention, and then I find it: Amedeo Modigliani and Jeanne Hébuterne. The joint grave is highlighted with flowers and someone has left a charcoal crayon as a tribute to Modigliani's art. Somewhere under the stone lie the remains of an artist who inspired the artist who is the subject of this book. Thousands and thousands of miles away, an awkward girl in New Jersey began a journey because of the man who is buried in front of me now – as others have done and will do because of Patti Smith.

Discography

ALBUMS

Patti Smith
Horses (Arista) 1975
Gloria (Part 1: In Excelsis Deo; Part 2: Gloria), Redondo
Beach, Birdland, Free Money, Kimberly, Break It Up, Land
(Part 1: Horses, Part 2: Land Of A Thousand Dances, Part 3:
La Mer [De]), Elegie.
CD bonus track: My Generation (live)

Patti Smith Group
Radio Ethiopia (Arista) 1976
Ask The Angels, Ain't It Strange, Poppies, Pissing In The
River, Pumping (My Heart), Distant Fingers, Radio
Ethiopia, Abyssinia
CD bonus track: Chicklets
Radio Ethiopia and Abyssinia were recorded live on
9 August, 1976.

Patti Smith Group
Easter (Arista) 1978
Till Victory, Space Monkey, Because The Night, Ghost
Dance, Babelogue, Rock'n'Roll Nigger, Privilege (Set Me
Free) with 23rd Psalm, We Three, 25th Floor, High On
Rebellion, Easter
CD bonus track: Godspeed

Patti Smith Group
Wave (Arista) 1979
Frederick, Dancing Barefoot, So You Want To Be A Rock

'N' Roll Star, Hymn, Revenge, Citizen Ship, Seven Ways
Of Going, Broken Flag, Wave
CD bonus tracks: Fire Of Unknown Origin and 5-4-3-2-1/
Wave

Patti Smith
Dream Of Life (Arista) 1988
People Have The Power, Going Under, Up There Down
There, Paths That Cross, Dream Of Life, Where Duty Calls,
Looking For You (I Was), The Jackson Song
CD bonus tracks: As the Night Goes By and Wild Leaves

Patti Smith
Gone Again (Arista) 1996
Gone Again, Beneath The Southern Cross, About A Boy,
My Madrigal, Summer Cannibals, Dead To The World,
Wing, Ravens, Wicked Messenger, Fireflies, Farewell Reel

The Patti Smith Masters (Arista) 1996
Box set of 20-bit digitally remastered editions of the first five
albums complete with original artwork, sleeve notes and
bonus tracks as listed above.

Patti Smith
Peace And Noise (Arista) 1997
Waiting Underground, Whirl Away, 1959, Spell, Don't Say
Nothing, Dead City, Blue Poles, Death Singing, Memento
Mori, Last Call

Patti Smith
Gung Ho (Arista) 2000
One Voice, Lo And Beholden, Boy Cried Wolf, Persuasion,
Gone Pie, China Bird, Glitter In Their Eyes, Strange
Messengers, Grateful, Upright Come, New Party, Libbie's
Song, Gung Ho.

Discography

Patti Smith
Land (1975–2002) (Arista) 2002
A two-CD collection featuring a compilation of previously released material on disc one and b-sides and unreleased material on disc two.

Patti Smith
Trampin' (Columbia) 2004
Jubilee, Mother Rose, Stride Of The Mind, Cartwheels, Gandhi, Trespasses, My Blakean Year, Cash, Peaceable Kingdom, Radio Baghdad, Trampin'.

Patti Smith
Horses / Horses (Sony) 2005
Two-CD collection featuring a digitally remastered version of the original studio album *Horses* on disc one and a live version of *Horses* played in its entirety recorded on June 25 2005 at the Meltdown Festival at London's Royal Festival Hall on disc two.

Patti Smith
Twelve (Columbia) 2007
Are You Experienced?, Everybody Wants To Rule The World, Helpless, Gimme Shelter, Within You Without You, White Rabbit, Changing Of The Guards, The Boy In The Bubble, Soul Kitchen, Smells Like Teen Spirit, Midnight Rider, Pastime Paradise.
Bonus track: Everybody Hurts.

Patti Smith, Kevin Shields
The Coral Sea (Pask) 2008
A two-CD set documenting three live performances in London of *The Coral Sea*, with Kevin Shields, in 2005/2006.

Patti Smith
Outside Society (Sony) 2011
An 18-track single disc compilation.

US SINGLES/EPS/12 SINGLES

Hey Joe (Version), Hey Joe/Piss Factory
Mer Records, 1974

Gloria, In Excelsis Deo/My Generation (Live Cleveland,
Ohio 26/1/76)
Arista, 1976

Hey Joe (Version)/Piss Factory
Sire, 1977

Because The Night/Godspeed
Arista, 1978

Frederick/Frederick (Live)
Arista, 1979

People Have The Power/Wild Leaves
Arista, 1988

People Have The Power/Wild Leaves/Where Duty Calls
Arista, 1988

Looking For You (I Was)/Up There Down There
Arista, 1988

UK SINGLES/EPS/12 SINGLES

Gloria/My Generation (Live)
Arista 12″ 45rpm, 1976

Because The Night/Godspeed
Arista, 1978

Set Free EP
Privilege (Set Me Free) with 23rd Psalm/Ask The

Discography

Angels/25th Floor (Live Version)/Babelfield
Arista, 1978

Frederick/Fire Of Unknown Origin
Arista. 1979

Dancing Barefoot/5-4-3-2-1/Wave
Arista, 1979

People Have The Power/Wild Leaves
Arista, 1988

Summer Cannibals (CD version 1): Summer Cannibals
/Come Back Little Sheba/Gone Again (Acoustic Live, Jools
Holland Show 8/6/96)/People Have The Power (LP
version)
Arista, 1996

Summer Cannibals (CD version 2): Summer Cannibals
/People Have The Power (Spoken Word Live, Jools
Holland Show)/Beneath The Southern Cross/Come On In
My Kitchen
Arista, 1996

Poetry Bibliography

Seventh Heaven (Telegraph Books, 1972)

Kodak (Middle Earth Press, 1972)

Witt (Gotham Book Mart, 1973)

The Night 1976 A Useless Death (Gotham Book Mart, 1978)

Ha!Ha!Houdini! (Gotham Book Mart) 1977

Babel (G.P. Putnam's) 1978

Early Work 1970–1979 (W.W. Norton) 1994

The Coral Sea (Norton & Company) 1996

Patti Smith: Complete Lyrics, Reflections And Notes For The Future (Doubleday) 1998

Strange Messenger: The Work Of Patti Smith (Andy Warhol Museum) 2003

Auguries Of Innocence (Ecco Press) 2005

Land 250 (Fondation Cartier pour l'art contemporain) 2008

Trois (Fondation Cartier pour l'art contemporain) 2008

Just Kids (Ecco press) 2010

Index

8/12(184106)